Science Fair

1/02

Science Fair Success in the Hardware Store

Titles in the *Science Fair Success* series

HOW TO ENTER AND WIN AN
INVENTION CONTEST
ISBN 0-7660-1173-9

HOW TO EXCEL IN SCIENCE
COMPETITIONS
REVISED AND UPDATED
ISBN 0-7660-1292-1

SCIENCE FAIR PROJECTS
INVESTIGATING EARTHWORMS
ISBN 0-7660-1291-3

SCIENCE FAIR SUCCESS
IN THE HARDWARE STORE
ISBN 0-7660-1287-5

SCIENCE FAIR SUCCESS
REVISED AND EXPANDED
ISBN 0-7660-1163-1

SCIENCE FAIR SUCCESS
USING THE INTERNET
ISBN 0-7660-1172-0

SCIENCE FAIR SUCCESS
USING SUPERMARKET PRODUCTS
ISBN 0-7660-1288-3

SCIENCE FAIR SUCCESS
WITH PLANTS
ISBN 0-7660-1170-4

SPORTS SCIENCE PROJECTS
THE PHYSICS OF BALLS IN MOTION
ISBN 0-7660-1174-7

Science Fair Success in the Hardware Store

Salvatore Tocci

Enslow Publishers, Inc.

40 Industrial Road   PO Box 38
Box 398   Aldershot
Berkeley Heights, NJ 07922   Hants GU12 6BP
USA   UK

http://www.enslow.com

Library of Congress Cataloging-in-Publication Data

Tocci, Salvatore.
     Science fair success in the hardware store / Salvatore Tocci.
        p. cm. — (Science fair success)
     Includes bibliographical references and index.
     Summary: Presents experiments and related projects showing the science behind items
found in a hardware store, covering such topics as atomic structure, electricity, chemical
bonds, magnetism, and water analysis.
     ISBN 0-7660-1287-5
     1. Science projects Juvenile literature. [1. Science—Experiments. 2. Science projects.
3. Experiments.] I. Title. II. Series.
     Q182.3.T63   2000
     507'.8—dc21   99-35531
                                           CIP

Printed in the United States of America

10 9 8 7 6 5 4 3 2 1

To Our Readers:
All Internet addresses in this book were active and appropriate when we went to press. Any
comments or suggestions can be sent by e-mail to Comments@enslow.com or to the address on
the back cover.

Illustration Credits: Stephen F. Delisle

Photo Credits: © Corel Corporation

Cover Photo: © TSM/George B. Diebold

Contents

Introduction

You may think that science is a subject that is taught only in school or a topic that is investigated in a laboratory. But science is much more than this. Science is an important part of your daily life. No matter where you are, science has an impact on what you are doing. Even your home can be considered a laboratory where scientific principles are always at work. This book will give you the opportunity to examine another place where science can be explored—the hardware store.

You probably have been in a hardware store a number of times, most likely to buy something that you needed at home. Perhaps you purchased some potting soil to grow plants, a lightbulb for the kitchen, nails to build a tree house, a washer to stop a leaky faucet in the bathroom, or a thermometer to measure the outdoor temperature. Now you can visit a hardware store to purchase items to use in a science project. This book will show you how the gardening, electrical, building, plumbing, and recreational supply sections of your hardware store contain numerous items for you to use. Most of these items are inexpensive. In fact, you may already have many of them at home.

Experiments versus Science Projects

As you progress through this book, you will first be given some information about the science behind a particular product that you can find in a hardware store. You will then be shown how to carry out an *experiment* with that product. Using the materials that you found in the hardware store, you can then carry out the experiments described in this book right in your home. After finishing the experiment, you will sometimes read about an idea for a science *project* that is related to the product. You will need to do more thinking and planning and spend more time and effort on a science project as compared to an experiment. In some cases, an idea for a project will involve a product that you may not find in a hardware store but that you can locate either at home or in school. In every case, this book will give you the background you need to *start* the science project. You must then do some research to get additional information required to *carry out* the project. You can use your school or local library, check with your science teacher, or search the Internet. The sections in the back of this book list sites on the World Wide Web where you might start your Internet search, books that provide additional background information, and suppliers where you can purchase materials for your project.

Keep in mind that this book is only an introduction to experiments and science projects that you can perform with items sold in hardware stores. Do not be limited by what is written here. Use what you learn and your imagination to come up with ideas for additional experiments and projects. Perhaps something you do with a particular product in one chapter can be used with a different product mentioned in another chapter. Also do not be afraid to vary the procedures that are given. For example, if the procedure calls for seeing what happens when you heat something, you may want to experiment a little further. You can check to see what happens when the same thing is cooled. If you do decide to vary a procedure, first ask a knowledgeable adult to look over your project plans.

Designing an Experiment

If you decide to follow up one of the suggestions for a project described in this book, be sure you know what to do if your procedure involves designing an experiment. All experiments require a control. This does not mean that the person has total control over what is going into the experiment. Rather a control means that the experimenter designs the procedure so that what happens can likely be explained. Consider a simple experiment. Assume that you drop a chemical into a blue-colored liquid. The liquid turns yellow. You conclude that the chemical caused the liquid to change color. This seems to be a valid conclusion. However, someone could argue that the liquid changed color for another reason. Perhaps the light, temperature, or air in the room was responsible for the change in color. Although these causes seem unlikely, they might be responsible for what happened.

A better design for this experiment would involve two liquid samples. The chemical is added to one. Nothing is done to the other. Both are exposed to the same conditions. If the one with the chemical turns yellow, then you can justifiably conclude that the chemical was responsible for the color change. The liquid to which nothing was added served as the control. A **control** is an experimental design that allows only one factor—in this case the chemical—to affect what happens. By including the proper controls, an experimenter is able to pinpoint what causes a certain result to happen. So if you design an experiment, be sure to set it up so that you can identify the factor responsible for whatever happens.

The factor is known as a variable. A **variable** is something that changes. In the experiment with the colored liquid, the chemical added is known as an independent variable. An **independent variable** is a factor that the experimenter decides to add or change as part of the procedure. The experimenter is free or independent to test anything to see if it causes the solution to change color. On the other hand, the change in color is known as a dependent variable. A **dependent variable** is a factor that changes in response to what is done in the experiment. It depends on what the experimenter does. The solution changed from blue to yellow because of the chemical that was added to the liquid. If your experimental procedure involves a control, be sure to know what the independent and dependent variables are.

Keep in mind that all experiments require controls except for those that are demonstrations. To be sure if yours does, you can check with your science teacher. But before you actually carry out any experiment that you have designed, keep one important point in mind. First check with an adult to be sure that the procedure you have developed does not involve anything that might be dangerous or hazardous. Whenever a procedure or chemical that might be dangerous or hazardous crops up in this book, you will be reminded to have an adult supervise your work. In such cases, ask an adult to supervise your work as you carry out the experiment. In that way, you will not get hurt while you are doing your experiments.

No matter how simple or complex the procedure that is used in an experiment, be sure to observe safety procedures.

Always wear safety goggles, avoid touching chemicals, never place flammable substances near a flame, and know what you are doing at all times. Never eat or drink while you are carrying out an experiment. The safest bet is to follow the instructions in this book for each experiment, which include all the necessary precautions. If you are in doubt about anything, check with your science teacher or other adult.

The purpose of this book is to show you that science can be found anywhere, including a hardware store. All that you need to supply is an interest in finding out about the science that exists in a hardware store. One final note: Have fun!

Chapter 1

Gardening Supplies

Have you ever grown or helped to maintain a vegetable or flower garden? If you have, then you may have gone to your local hardware store to buy some gardening supplies. Perhaps you purchased some potting soil, fertilizer, or pesticide for your garden. Whatever was not used up last season may have been stored in the garage or basement. Now is the time to dig it back out, not for planting, but for experimenting. You can carry out a variety of interesting experiments and projects with gardening supplies, starting with potting soil.

Soil

Soil can be considered a chemical factory. Containing almost every known chemical element, soil is a mixture of minerals, salts, nutrients, gases dissolved in water, and organic compounds derived from animal wastes and decayed plants. More chemicals are added to the soil whenever fertilizers or pesticides are applied. Also, the weathering action of the sun, rain, and wind causes the erosion of small rocks and stones. Erosion releases more minerals and salts into the soil. With such a rich supply of chemicals, the soil is fertile ground for a variety of chemical reactions, all hidden beneath the surface of the earth.

One additional ingredient, however, is needed for all these reactions to occur—water. Without water, the chemical richness of the soil would be useless for growing anything. Most of the water that enters the soil comes from rain. In times of drought, a garden hose may be the source of water. But whether the water comes from the sky or a garden hose, often most of it drains away and does not get into the soil. Only a small amount that touches the ground may actually seep into the soil. The drier the soil and the flatter its surface, the more water can seep into the ground. However, the water not only must get into the ground but also must be retained by the soil for those times when it does not rain or when you forget to water your garden. The quantity of water that is retained by the soil depends on the soil's mineral composition.

For example, soil containing a high percentage of sand and gravel allows water to penetrate easily. But this type of soil does not retain the water well. Instead, the water quickly passes down into deeper layers, carrying with it many of the nutrients needed for plant growth. On the other hand, soil with a high silt or clay content does not allow water to penetrate as easily. However, this type of soil retains water very well, like a dry sponge that easily soaks up water. As a result, such soils retain the water and dissolved nutrients, preventing their use by plants. With so much water, these soils become soggy and do not promote good growing conditions.

Experiment 1.1

How Much Loam Is in Your Soil?

What is the best soil for growing plants? Both potting soil and commercial topsoil are good. Both these soils have a high content of loam. **Loam** is a mixture of several substances, including sand, clay, gravel, and silt, that are combined in the proper proportions for supporting plant growth. Many of the substances in loam are intermediate in size between the coarse particles in gravel and the very fine grains in clay and silt. These intermediate particles are called colloids. A **colloid** is a particle that is too large to dissolve in water and too small to settle to the bottom of a solution. Instead, colloids remain evenly distributed throughout a solution.

Materials

* soil samples
* potting soil
* tall, narrow drinking glass or graduated cylinder
* metric ruler
* masking tape
* marking pen
* small flashlight
* glass jar
* water
* measuring cup
* newspaper
* pencil
* balance

The colloids in soil function as a reservoir. When conditions are wet, these colloids retain much of the water that enters the soil. When conditions are dry, the colloids in loam slowly release the water and dissolved nutrients that they have held. Plants depend largely on this water that is released from colloids in the soil. Is there enough loam in your soil to provide the ideal growing conditions for plants?

Collect soil samples from different areas in your neighborhood. For example, samples can be taken from a garden, lawn, wooded area, or fields. If different types of soil are not readily available, you can take samples from different depths in the same area. Each sample should consist of enough soil to half fill a tall, narrow drinking glass. If you do not have any potting soil, get some at a hardware store to test.

With masking tape and a marking pen, draw two lines on a tall, narrow drinking glass. Place one near the middle and the other near the top. You could also use a graduated cylinder. Fill the glass with soil to the middle line. Be sure that the soil is dry and not wet or damp from a recent rainstorm. Slowly add water to the top line. Place your hand over the glass and shake vigorously for two minutes. Allow the glass to remain undisturbed overnight. As the soil settles in the glass, three distinct layers may form, as shown in Figure 1. Use a ruler to measure the height of each layer.

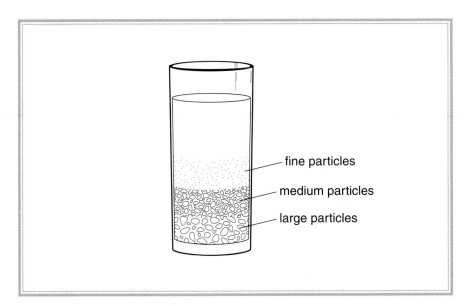

Figure 1. Upon settling, a soil sample mixed with water may separate into three distinct layers. The particles found in the middle layer are best for adsorbing and releasing water that is needed by plants.

Calculate the percent that each layer represents of the total soil sample. For example, if the layer of fine particles measures 2 centimeters (cm) and the height of the entire soil sample is 10 cm, then the percentage of fine particles in the soil is 2 cm/10 cm or 20 percent.

Is the liquid layer above the soil sample clear or cloudy? To test for the presence of colloids in this layer, shine a beam from a flashlight through this liquid layer. Describe what you see. If no colloids are present, then the light beam will pass straight through the liquid, and you will not see the beam in the water within the glass. However, if colloids are present, they will scatter the light, so that the beam is visible as it passes through the liquid. This effect on light by colloidal particles is known as the *Tyndall effect*, which is illustrated in Figure 2.

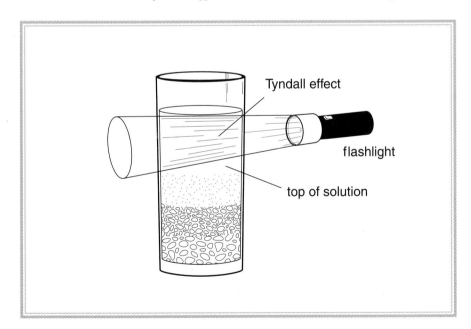

Figure 2. Use a tiny flashlight to shine a beam of light at a liquid. If colloids are present, they will scatter the light so that the beam is visible within the liquid. This is known as the Tyndall effect.

The greater the Tyndall effect, the more colloids present. The more colloids present, the higher the loam content of the soil.

You can also check the soil samples for their ability to adsorb water. But first you must be sure that the soil is thoroughly dry. Spread out the soil on a piece of newspaper and dry it in the sun for several days. Use a pencil to stir the soil several times a day to be sure that it completely dries. Place the dried soil in the glass up to the top line. Fill a measuring cup with water. Slowly add the water to the soil. Determine the volume of water that can be added before any rises above

Project Idea

Use Soil to Make an All-Natural Fertilizer

If you need some fertilizer for your indoor house plants, try making it from your garden soil. All you have to do is suspend some soil in cheesecloth above a large pail. Use string to secure the cheesecloth to the rim of the pail. Slowly pour tap water through the soil, as shown in Figure 3. When the water has finished dripping through the soil, remove the cheesecloth and pour the water into another container. Replace the cheesecloth on the pail. Pour the water that you collected in the container through the soil. Repeat this procedure several times. As the water passes through the soil, it will dissolve and wash out nutrients that are present, causing the water to turn murky. This process of dissolving and washing out nutrients is known as leaching. Thus, the water that is rich in nutrients is called a *leachate*. Use your leachate as a fertilizer. Test different soil samples to see which produces the leachate that is the best fertilizer.

the soil. This represents the volume of water that the soil can adsorb. Keep this soil sample for the next step.

Check the soil samples for their ability to retain water. Weigh the soil sample, water, and glass from the previous step. Place the glass near a window. As the water evaporates, the weight of the sample will decrease. Continue weighing the sample each day until no further decrease in weight is noted. The longer it takes for all the water to evaporate, the better the ability of the soil to retain water. Any soil sample that cannot adsorb water well or retain it for very long will not be much good for growing plants.

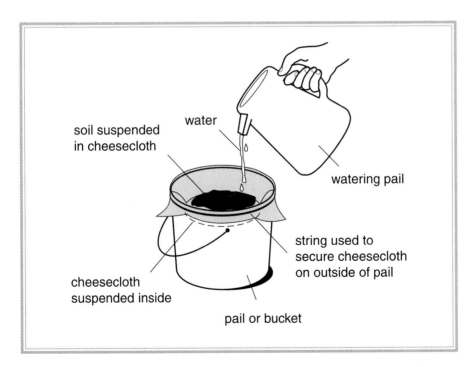

soil suspended in cheesecloth

water

watering pail

string used to secure cheesecloth on outside of pail

cheesecloth suspended inside

pail or bucket

Figure 3. Cheesecloth is handy for filtering solutions. In this case, the cheesecloth traps the soil but allows the water and dissolved nutrients to pass into the pail.

Experiment 1.2

What Is the pH of Your Soil?

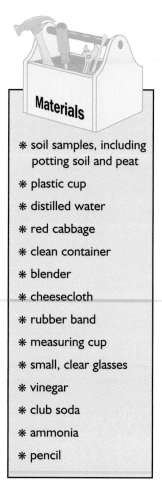

The colloidal particles in soil not only affect its moisture content but also its acidity level. As materials dissolve in water, the resulting solution can be either acidic, neutral, or basic. One way to determine what type of solution is formed is by measuring its pH. The **pH** of a solution is a measurement of the relative strength of an acid or base. As you can see in Figure 4, the pH value can range from 0 to 14. Anything with a pH value of 7 is considered neutral. Distilled water, which is 100 percent pure water, has a pH value of 7. By the way, some of the experiments and projects described in this book call for the use of distilled water. Check with your science teacher if it is possible to make distilled water in school. If not, you can purchase distilled water at a hardware store.

Anything with a pH value lower than 7 is classified as an acid; the stronger the acid, the lower its pH value. Thus an **acid** can be defined as a substance that produces a solution with a pH value less than 7. Acidic solutions that you might have at home include vinegar, orange juice, and carbonated

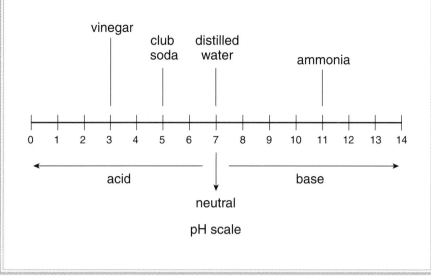

Figure 4. On the pH scale, the strongest acid has a pH value of 0, and the strongest base has a pH value of 14. Anything with a pH value of 7 is considered neutral.

beverages. Anything with a pH value greater than 7 is classified as a base; the stronger the base, the higher its pH value. Thus a **base** can be defined as a substance that produces a solution with a pH value greater than 7. Basic, or alkaline, solutions that you might have at home include ammonia and liquid drain cleaners.

The pH value is a mathematical function. Each unit on the pH scale represents a tenfold difference in concentration. Thus an acid solution with a pH of 4 is ten times more concentrated an acid than a solution with a pH of 5. A solution with a pH of 4 is also one hundred times more concentrated an acid than a solution with a pH of 6. Which is the more concentrated base—a solution with a pH value of 12 or one with a pH value of 9? How much more concentrated a base is it?

Soils can be either acidic or alkaline. Alkaline soils are found primarily in the arid regions of the western United States. On the other hand, soils in areas where conifers, such as pine and fir trees, grow are acidic. Chemicals released from decaying conifer needles that fall to the ground in the autumn cause the soil to become even more acidic. This high acidity level is fine for these types of trees. However, such a soil is too acidic for most vegetable and plant gardens. Most vegetables and plants prefer a pH between 5 and 7. Within this range, many of the nutrients can be released from the colloidal particles in soil, making them available to the plants. Some plants, however, thrive best in an acidic soil. These plants include magnolias, holly bushes, azaleas, and gardenias.

If the soil is too acidic for the plants that you want to grow, a base can be added. This practice is commonly referred to as "sweetening the soil." Most often soil is sweetened by the addition of lime, which is a base and usually sold by hardware stores in large bags. The amount of lime that needs to be added depends on how acidic the soil is. You can use the juice extracted from red cabbage to check the pH of your soil.

Tear the leaves from a red cabbage into small pieces. Place the pieces into a blender and cover with distilled water. **Under adult supervision,** blend the leaves until they have liquefied. Filter the cabbage juice through cheesecloth and collect the liquid in a clean container, as shown in Figure 5. The cabbage juice contains an indicator. An **indicator** is a chemical substance that changes color, depending on the pH of the solution.

Pour 25 milliliters (mL), which is about 1 fluid ounce, of the juice into a small, clear glass. Add 25 mL of vinegar, which has a pH value of about 3. What color does the vinegar turn?

Label and save this solution. Repeat this procedure, this time adding 25 mL of club soda, which has a pH value of about 5, into another small glass. What color does the cabbage juice turn? Label and save this solution. Follow the same procedure, using 25 mL of distilled water and 25 mL of ammonia, which has a pH of about 11. **Do not spill or inhale the ammonia.**

Take a soil sample from your garden or lawn and place it in a clean, dry plastic cup. Add enough distilled water (at least 50 mL) to moisten the soil. Mix the soil and water by stirring with a pencil. Allow the soil to settle, then stir again. Do this several times. After the soil has settled, carefully pour 25 mL of the water into a small, clear glass. Add 25 mL of cabbage juice and compare the color to the others that you obtained with the club soda, vinegar, distilled water, and ammonia.

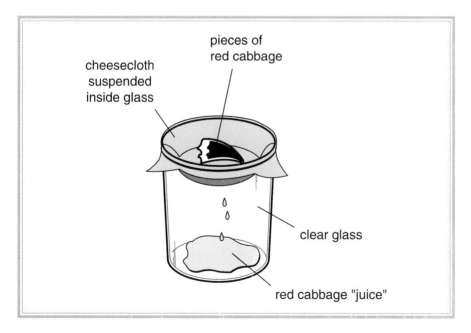

Figure 5. The red cabbage "juice" that collects in the container can be used to determine the pH of a solution.

What is the pH of your soil? If the color of the red cabbage solution falls between the one with the club soda and the one with vinegar, then you can conclude that the pH of your soil sample is about 4. What would be the pH of the soil sample if the color of the red cabbage solution is somewhere between the one of distilled water and the one with ammonia?

If the pH of your soil is too acidic for your vegetable or plant garden, determine how much lime you must add by checking at the hardware store. Be sure to inform them of the pH value of your soil and the types of vegetables or plants that you intend to grow.

Acid Precipitation

The pH of rain is naturally acidic, with a value of about 5.4. In recent years, concerns have been raised about the increasing acidity of soils, lakes, streams, ponds, and rivers. This increase is the result of acid precipitation, which includes acid rain, snow, and sleet. The most acidic rainfall in the United States occurred in Wheeling, West Virginia, where the pH was measured at 1.5.

Acid precipitation develops, in part, from certain gases that are emitted into the atmosphere. These gases include carbon dioxide, sulfur dioxide, and nitrogen dioxide. The gases are released into the atmosphere mainly as a result of the burning of fossil fuels such as coal and oil. After they are released into the atmosphere, each of these gases reacts with the moisture in the air. These gases combine with water to produce acids, which then fall back to earth whenever it rains, snows, or sleets. The more gases released, the more acids formed, and the more acidic the precipitation.

Acid precipitation can have a wide impact. When present in the atmosphere, the acids contribute to haze. This affects visibility, making it more difficult for pilots to see. The haze also reduces the amount of sunlight that reaches the earth. This reduction in sunlight is felt mainly in the Arctic, where plants known as lichens are mostly affected. With less sunlight, these plants cannot grow as well. In turn, the caribou and reindeer that feed upon the lichens are affected.

When the acids in the atmosphere fall to earth as precipitation, they affect both nonliving and living things. Acids that fall upon statues and buildings cause corrosion. Upon prolonged exposure to acids, the limestone and marble used to build these structures turn into a crumbling substance called gypsum. Metals are also affected by acid precipitation. In 1967, a bridge over the Ohio River collapsed, killing forty-six people. Engineers discovered that the bridge collapsed because the metal used to build the bridge corroded as a result of acid precipitation.

Experiment 1.3

What Can Acid Precipitation Do?

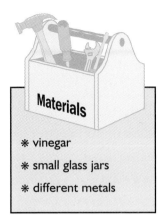

Materials

* vinegar
* small glass jars
* different metals

When a metal reacts with an acid that is present in precipitation, two products are usually formed. As you can see in Figure 6, one is a gas. The other is a salt that dissolves easily in water. Obviously, the metal is no longer present once it has reacted with acid. But not all metals react with acids in this way, as you can see in this experiment.

Check a hardware store to see how many different metals you can find. Some of the metals available in a hardware store include copper used in electrical wiring, iron found in nails, and zinc that is present as a thin layer on galvanized nails.

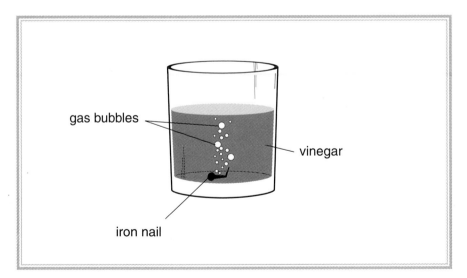

gas bubbles

vinegar

iron nail

Figure 6. Gas bubbles will be produced as long as there is metal to react with the acid in vinegar.

Place each type of metal in a glass jar and cover it with vinegar. Notice whether the metal reacts with the acid present in vinegar. Make periodic observations over twenty-four hours. Which metals react the quickest with the acid? Prepare a list of metals, starting with the most active and progressing down to those that do not react with acid. Expand your observations to test the reaction of alloys with acid. An **alloy** is a combination of two or more metals that can be either a solid or a liquid. Brass, for example, is mainly a mixture of copper and zinc. Which metal, do you conclude, is most easily affected by acid precipitation? Which metal would you use to build a bridge?

Experiment 1.4

How Can You Turn Garbage into Fertilizer?

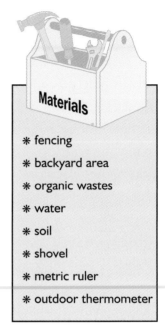

Materials

* fencing
* backyard area
* organic wastes
* water
* soil
* shovel
* metric ruler
* outdoor thermometer

Most people fertilize their gardens with products that are available at a hardware store. You might have even found some when you looked through what had been stored in your garage or basement. If you did find a bag of fertilizer, look at the label. You will see that fertilizer contains three main ingredients: nitrogen, phosphorus, and potassium. The nitrogen is present in a compound called ammonium nitrate. Most of phosphorus is provided by calcium dihydrogen phosphate, and the potassium is supplied by potassium carbonate. Manufacturers are required by law to label the percentage of each of the three main ingredients in their product. The percentages are indicated by a series of numbers. A fertilizer labeled 5-10-5 contains 5 percent nitrogen, 10 percent phosphorus, and 5 percent potassium (potash).

When fertilizer is needed, many gardeners prefer adding organic material prepared from decayed matter instead of commercial products that contain inorganic compounds. With a few exceptions, **organic compounds** are ones that contain the element carbon. As a rule, **inorganic compounds** lack carbon. Recall that commercial fertilizers contain the elements nitrogen, phosphorus, and potassium. If organic matter is used for fertilizing, then a person can claim that all the plants have been grown using only natural conditions and ingredients. The organic matter can be obtained from one of four sources: compost, animal manure, fish-oil products, and seaweed. Compost is the most commonly used organic fertilizer. One reason is that making compost is rather simple.

Select an area that can be fenced in for making the compost. The fencing material must allow air to circulate but prevent scattering by the wind or animals. Check a hardware store for the proper type of fencing. The area that you fence in can be as small or as large as you want.

Add organic wastes to a depth of 25 cm (10 in) to start the compost pile. You can use leaves and grass cuttings that are mixed with food wastes. Food wastes that you can use include fruit and vegetable remains, eggshells, coffee grinds, potato skins, and stale bread. Now you can truly say that even the food wastes in your house are not being wasted!

Cover the wastes with at least 10 cm (4 in) of soil. Bacteria in the soil will break down the organic wastes into nutrients that plants can use. Keep the compost pile moist but not too wet. If the compost pile emits an unpleasant odor, then add less water. Repeat the layering of 25 cm of organic wastes and 10 cm of soil, as shown in Figure 7.

Allow the pile to remain undisturbed for six weeks. Add water when necessary. You may notice that the compost pile gets hot. The chemical reactions that are breaking down the organic wastes release energy in the form of heat. Stick an outdoor thermometer in the pile to see how hot it actually gets. After six weeks, the pile should be turned with a shovel to promote contact between the bacteria and organic matter that has

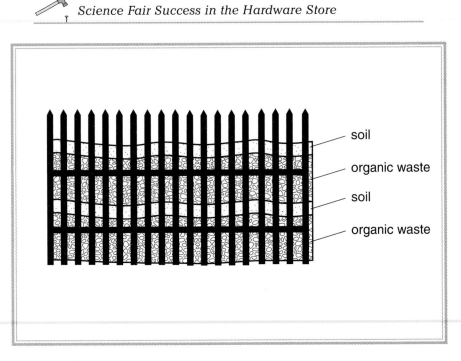

soil

organic waste

soil

organic waste

Figure 7. Be sure that your fencing does not allow the compost to escape but does allow air to circulate. Notice how organic wastes are alternately layered with soil.

not yet decomposed. A second compost area is most helpful. Remove the top layer from the first area and place it on the bottom of the second area. Continue this process until all the layers have been inverted.

The compost is ready when a small sample crumbles in your hand. Spread about 10 cm (4 in) of compost over the garden area and then work it into the soil. Several applications of compost are best, all done preferably before planting time. By that time, your garden will be rich in nutrients that have been prepared from your household garbage. You can compare how plants grow in the compost compared with your regular garden soil that contains no compost. Which plants grow larger? Which plants produce more flowers?

Experiment 1.5

How Can You Get Rid of Just the Pests?

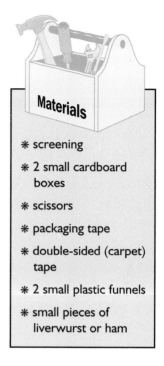

Materials

* screening
* 2 small cardboard boxes
* scissors
* packaging tape
* double-sided (carpet) tape
* 2 small plastic funnels
* small pieces of liverwurst or ham

Every gardener worries about pests such as beetles, caterpillars, and moths that can destroy their vegetables or plants. To prevent their gardens from being attacked by such pests, gardeners often resort to using pesticides. The next time you are in the hardware store, check to see what kinds of pesticides are sold. Unfortunately, pesticides also kill other animals that pose no threat to a person's garden. However, there is something other than a pesticide that eliminates just the pests.

As an alternative to pesticides, gardeners sometimes use pheromones. A **pheromone** is a chemical that is released by an animal to communicate with others through scent or taste. Some pheromones attract members of the opposite sex. Traps containing a pheromone are set up to lure and capture a pest before it has a chance to do any damage. Once inside, the pest cannot escape because it sticks to a glue that is added to the trap. Different pheromone traps are available, each designed to attract and capture a particular pest. Check to see what pheromone products are sold as pesticides in the gardening supply section of your local hardware store. This experiment shows you how to build a trap that mimics the action of a pheromone. **Do not do this experiment if you are allergic to bee stings.**

Use a scissors to remove the tops of 2 small, cardboard boxes. Cover the bottoms of the boxes with double-sided tape. Then cut 2 pieces of screening and bend the edges so that they fit over the cardboard boxes. Secure the screening to the boxes with packaging tape. Use the scissors to poke a small hole through the screening. The hole should be large enough to support a small funnel, as shown in Figure 8. Be sure that the stem of the funnel is wide enough so that a bee can pass through it. In one box, remove the funnel and drop several small pieces of liverwurst or ham into the box. Add nothing

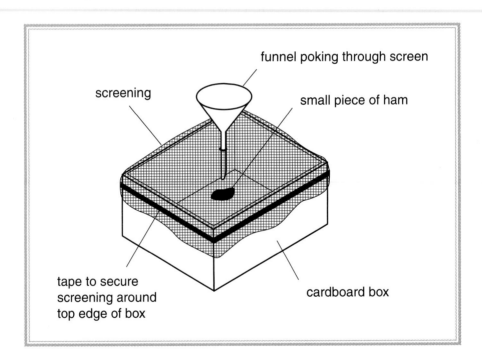

screening

funnel poking through screen

small piece of ham

tape to secure screening around top edge of box

cardboard box

Figure 8. The odor given off by the meat will attract insects, including yellow jackets. Be very careful whenever you are near the trap so that you do not get stung by the bees. Ask an adult to dispose of the trap when you are finished with your experiment.

to the second box; this is your control. Replace the funnels and set the traps outdoors.

The meat will act as a pheromone, attracting any yellow jackets that are in the area. Experiment with different foods to see which ones work best in attracting yellow jackets. You can try fish, canned cat food, jelly, and fruit juice. Be sure to **ask an adult** to help you dispose of any traps that contain yellow jackets. Does your "pheromone" trap capture more bees than the trap with no added food? If so, you may want to join the group of scientists who are searching for more effective pheromone traps. Start by checking the Internet for information, using "pheromone" as your keyword to begin your search.

Chapter 2

Electrical Supplies

Do you recall a time when you touched someone or something and got a mild shock? Or how about a time when you combed your hair and it would not stay down? Perhaps you have had articles of clothing cling together after they were removed from the dryer. All these things happened because of something called static electricity. Just what is static electricity? To understand what static electricity is, you must first know what electricity is. And to understand what electricity is, you must know something about the structure of atoms.

Atomic Structure

An **atom** is the unit from which all matter is made. Atoms are too small to be seen with the naked eye. In fact, they are so small that it takes over a million atoms to form something the size of the period at the end of this sentence. Greek philosophers living around 400 B.C. were the first to suggest that atoms exist. Only recently have scientists been able to see an atom, with the help of a very powerful microscope. Even without seeing one, scientists were still able to discover much about atoms.

For example, they discovered that an atom consists of three basic particles: a proton, neutron, and an electron. The protons and neutrons are contained in a tightly knit core region known as the *nucleus*. A **proton** carries a positive charge, a **neutron** is neutral, and an **electron** carries a negative charge. The electrons travel around the nucleus, somewhat like the planets orbiting the sun. But unlike the planets, the electrons sometimes leave their orbits to join another atom.

Electricity

Electricity is a form of energy that is generated whenever electrons flow from one object or chemical to another. Usually the electrons flow through a metal wire. The wire is said to be a **conductor** because it allows electrons to be easily conducted, or passed through it. Metals are excellent conductors because they readily allow electrons to flow between their atoms. Other substances and objects do not conduct electricity well and are called **insulators**. What materials sold in your local hardware store are good electrical conductors? Good electrical insulators?

Metals are not the only electrical conductors that allow electrons to flow. In fact, whenever two different objects come in close contact, electrons may be spontaneously transferred from one to the other. In this case, the transfer of electrons from one object to another is known as static electricity. **Static electricity** is generated whenever electrons spontaneously jump from one object to another. To generate static electricity, rub one balloon with a wool cloth and a second balloon with plastic wrap. Hold the balloons close together and observe what happens. Next rub one balloon with a wool cloth and the other with a piece of silk. Again observe what happens when the two balloons are brought together.

In the first case, the balloons came together because of static electricity. Wool is a material that readily gives up electrons. Rubbing with a wool cloth produces an excess of electrons on the balloon. With more electrons, this balloon becomes negatively charged, as shown in Figure 9a. Plastic wrap is a material that readily takes electrons. Rubbing with plastic wrap results in a deficiency of electrons on the balloon.

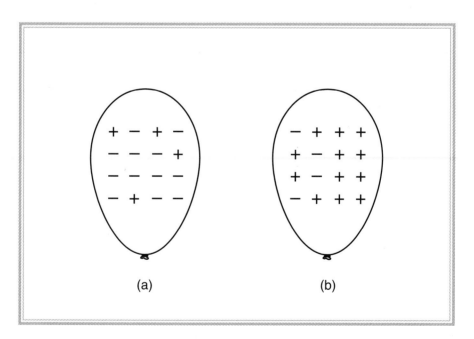

(a)   (b)

Figure 9. a) When rubbed with a wool cloth, a balloon becomes covered by electrons with their negative charges. b) When rubbed with plastic wrap, a balloon loses electrons and thus has more positive charges. These two balloons will then attract each other.

With fewer electrons, this balloon becomes positively charged, as shown in Figure 9b. Materials with opposite charges attract each other, so the two balloons came together. Electrons then jump from the balloon rubbed with wool to the balloon rubbed with plastic wrap, generating static electricity.

What must have happened to the balloon rubbed with a piece of silk to cause it to move away from the balloon rubbed with wool? Why do electrons not flow from one balloon to the other in this case? If you want to see something very unusual, rub a balloon with a wool cloth and then hold it near a mixture of salt and pepper spread out on a table. If you can explain what happens, then you really understand static electricity!

Experiment 2.1

How Can You Establish a Flow of Electrons?

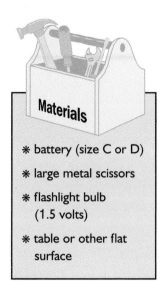

Materials

❋ battery (size C or D)

❋ large metal scissors

❋ flashlight bulb (1.5 volts)

❋ table or other flat surface

Batteries contain chemical compounds that cause electrons to flow, generating electrical energy. One chemical compound in the battery gives up its electrons to another chemical compound. But the battery is constructed in such a way that electrons cannot flow directly from one compound to another. Instead, the electrons flow through a conductor that is attached to the battery, as shown in Figure 10. This flow of electrons supplies the electrical energy that runs your portable CD player or powers your remote control. This experiment will show you how a pair of scissors can allow electrons to flow.

Place a battery (size C or D) so that its side rests on a table or other flat surface. Refer to Figure 11. Open a pair of large, metal scissors and touch one tip of a blade to the bottom of the battery or negative end, which is labeled with a - sign. Place the tip of the other blade near the top of the battery or positive end, which is labeled with a + sign. Hold a 1.5-volt flashlight bulb so that its metal end touches both the top of the battery and the tip of the blade. Use both hands to keep everything touching. Notice what happens to the bulb.

The blades of the scissors act as conductors, allowing electrons to flow in the direction shown by the arrows in

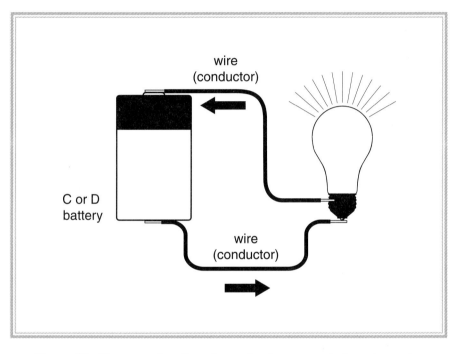

wire
(conductor)

C or D
battery

wire
(conductor)

Figure 10. Electrons that flow from the battery and through a wire generate electrical energy that lights the bulb. To complete the circuit, the electrons return to the battery through another piece of wire. Thus, the wire acts as a conductor by allowing electrons to flow.

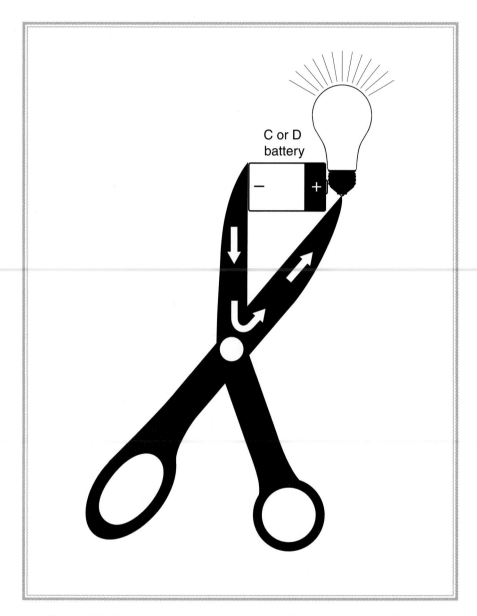

Figure 11. A pair of metal scissors completes the circuit, allowing electricity to flow and light the bulb.

Figure 11. Once the blades are positioned, an electric circuit is established. What would happen if you "shorted" the circuit by removing one end of the scissors? Look around your house to see what else besides scissors will serve as a conductor. Which one is the best? How could you tell? Is there anything in your house that is a good insulator? You can experiment by inserting various objects between the tip of the blade and the lightbulb. Anything that causes the lightbulb not to glow is an insulator.

Experiment 2.2

How Can You Turn a Fruit into a Battery?

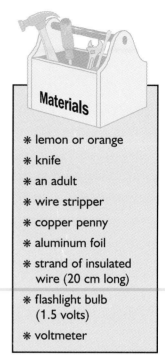

Materials

* lemon or orange
* knife
* an adult
* wire stripper
* copper penny
* aluminum foil
* strand of insulated wire (20 cm long)
* flashlight bulb (1.5 volts)
* voltmeter

Now that you know what a battery does, you should be able to make your own. Like any other battery, the one you will make contains electrolytes. An **electrolyte** is any substance in a solution that conducts an electric current. For example, the battery in your car contains a group of lead plates immersed in a solution of sulfuric acid. The sulfuric acid serves as the electrolyte, allowing the electrons to flow from one lead plate to another. This flow of electrons generates the electrical energy that starts the engine.

In this experiment, you can put together some simple items to make a battery out of a lemon or orange. Because sulfuric acid is a strong acid and can cause severe skin burns, you will instead use the weak citric acid in fruits to serve as the electrolyte.

Ask an adult to make two parallel slits with a sharp knife in a lemon or orange. Insert the copper penny in one slit and a piece of aluminum foil that has been folded in several layers in the other slit. Make sure that the penny and foil extend out from the surface of the fruit.

Cut a 20-cm strand of insulated wire in half. Use a wire stripper to remove the insulation from both ends of each wire. Take one wire and poke one end through the aluminum foil

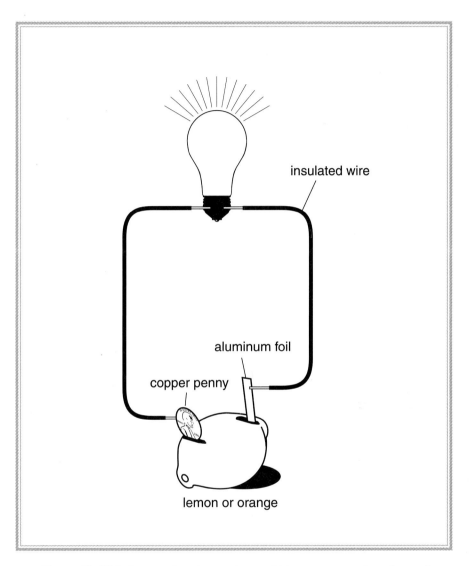

insulated wire

aluminum foil

copper penny

lemon or orange

Figure 12. This battery is a lemon into which a penny and a piece of aluminum foil have been inserted. What other citrus fruits will conduct an electric current?

that you inserted into the piece of fruit. **Ask an adult** to hold one end of the other wire to the penny. Then take the free ends of both wires and touch them to the bulb, as shown in Figure 12. Observe what happens.

Electrons flow from the aluminum strip, through the wire causing the bulb to light, and then flow to the copper metal in the penny. The juice inside the fruit contains electrolytes that help to keep electrons flowing. Experiment with different metals such as zinc, iron, nickel, tin, and lead, to determine which pair is most effective in establishing an electric current. Check the hardware store to see what kinds of metal nails they sell. Also try different citrus fruits to see if they vary in their capacity to function as electrolytes. Use the brightness of the bulb as an indication of how well the metals and electrolytes allow electrons to flow.

How Much Voltage Does Your Fruit Generate?

Different types of batteries supply different voltages. **Voltage** can be thought of as an "electrical pressure." Pressure refers to the force that is acting or pressing upon something. In the case of voltage, the pressure is caused by electrons. Both the negative and positive ends of a battery are made of metal, and both ends contain electrons. But the negative end contains a greater concentration of electrons. You can think of voltage in this way: The greater concentration of electrons at the negative end of a battery is the result of "electrical pressure" pushing electrons away from the positive end and into the negative end. The greater the push, the higher the voltage. As you may know, voltage is measured in volts.

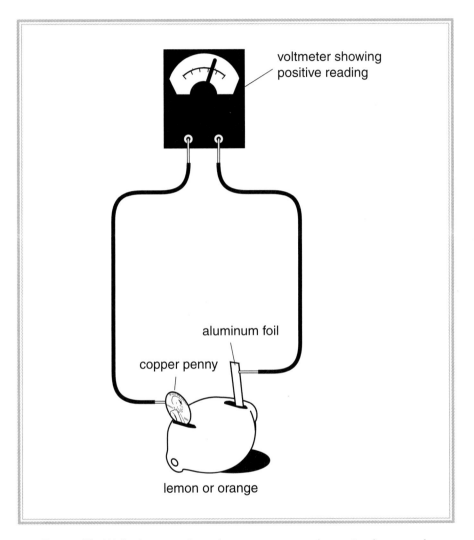

voltmeter showing positive reading

aluminum foil

copper penny

lemon or orange

Figure 13. With the use of a voltmeter, you can determine how much voltage your battery generates. Be sure to connect the wires to the voltmeter so that you get a positive reading.

Mercury batteries supply 1.34 volts, which is suitable for use in communication equipment and scientific instruments. An alkaline D battery provides 1.5 volts. Two of these batteries, when connected, provide 3 volts, which is enough electricity to power a flashlight. To provide the electrical energy needed to start a car, a lead-acid battery provides 12 volts. You can determine how much voltage your fruit battery generates by using a voltmeter. You can probably find an inexpensive voltmeter in the electrical supply section of your hardware store.

Using the same battery you already constructed, connect the wires to a voltmeter rather than a bulb. Connect them so that you get a positive value reading on the voltmeter, as shown in Figure 13. What voltage is generated by your battery? Experiment with different metals to see what voltages are produced. Does one type of fruit consistently supply the highest voltage readings?

Project Idea

Galvanic versus Electrolytic Cells

A battery is a galvanic cell, in which chemical energy is converted into electrical energy. A new type of battery that is becoming increasingly popular is the rechargeable type. Although they cost more than a regular battery, the fact that they can be reused many times saves money in the long run. Just how much money do they save? Design a project to find out.

When a rechargeable battery is being used, it operates as a galvanic cell, converting chemical energy into electrical energy. However, when it is being recharged, it operates as an electrolytic cell in which electrical energy is converted to chemical energy. An electrolytic cell is connected to an electrical energy source, such as another battery or some external source of electricity. As long as the electrolytic cell is connected, the electrical energy that is being supplied is converted into chemical energy. Once the chemical energy has been replenished, the battery can again operate as a galvanic cell. Check the library or search the Internet for information about galvanic and electrolytic cells. Prepare a report that summarizes the chemistry behind each type of cell.

You can also include information about fuel cells, which are a type of galvanic cell. In the case of fuel cells, which are used to provide electrical power aboard the space shuttle, a fuel is supplied from outside the cell. Much work is currently being done to develop fuel cells that can be used to build a new type of power plant. Most power plants currently in operation first convert chemical energy into heat energy. The heat energy is then converted into electrical energy. This process is not very efficient because little of the heat energy can be converted into electrical energy. Fuel cells convert chemical energy directly into electrical energy, bypassing the conversion to heat energy. Thus, fuel cells are much more efficient. Some countries, such as Japan, have constructed power plants that use fuel cells. Check the Internet for information on how these power plants are performing.

Experiment 2.3

How Can You Use Electrolysis to Create a Family Heirloom?

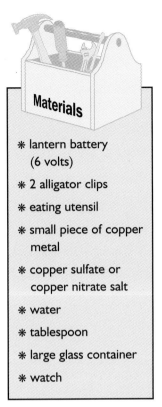

Materials

* lantern battery (6 volts)
* 2 alligator clips
* eating utensil
* small piece of copper metal
* copper sulfate or copper nitrate salt
* water
* tablespoon
* large glass container
* watch

Have you ever heard the term *electrolysis*? If you have, then it was most likely in the context of unwanted hair. Ads in magazines and newspapers advertise electrolysis as a way of removing hair from various body parts, especially the face. The process involves applying a mild electric current to kill the hair cell. **Electrolysis** is the use of electrical energy to produce a chemical change. Here is your chance to experiment with electrolysis, not to remove any hair that you may want to get rid of, but rather to see how it works.

You may have heard the term *silver-plated dinnerware*. Electrolytic cells are used to plate, or coat, a metal such as silver onto various objects, including spoons, knives, and forks. This process is known as **electroplating**, which is the use of electrical energy to produce a chemical change that involves coating an object with a pure metal. The following experiment will show you how to electroplate an eating utensil that you have at home. Be sure to select a utensil that can be thrown away if your project does not work properly.

Figure 14 shows how to set up the electroplating apparatus. You will need a battery that generates at least 6 volts. The positive terminal of the battery should be connected by an alligator clip to a strip of copper metal. The negative terminal of the battery should be connected by an alligator clip to the eating utensil.

Both the metal strip and eating utensil must be immersed in a solution that contains ions of the metal to be plated. For example, if copper is the metal to be plated, then the solution must contain copper ions. An **ion** is a charged particle that

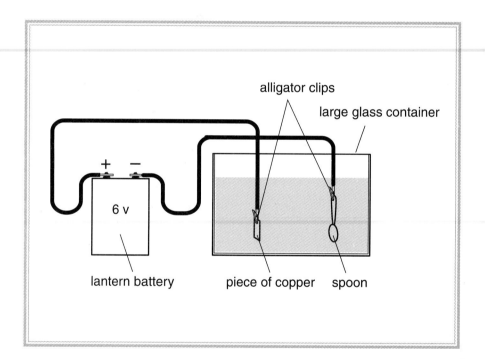

Figure 14. The battery supplies the energy that is needed to force electrons to flow and cause the utensil to become coated with a metal. If the battery were not attached, no flow of electrons would be established. You can use a pre-1983 penny as a source of copper. First clean the penny by soaking it for five minutes in a glass of vinegar mixed with a tablespoon of table salt. Rinse and dry the penny before wrapping the wire around it.

forms when an atom either loses or gains an electron. Copper ions have a positive charge.

Your science teacher probably has a salt that dissolves in water to produce copper ions. Such salts include copper sulfate and copper nitrate. Pour water into a large glass container so that it is three-quarters full. Add two tablespoons of the copper salt and stir the water until the salt completely dissolves.

Once everything is connected as shown in Figure 14, wait approximately five to seven minutes for the electroplating process to begin. The copper atoms that make up the metal strip will give up electrons. These electrons will be picked up by the eating utensil. The copper ions in solution with their positive charge will be attracted to the utensil as it gains negative charges. As a result, the copper ions will pick up the electrons to form copper atoms that plate the utensil. Notice what happens to the metal strip, the solution, and the eating utensil as the electroplating process continues. The utensil should become covered with copper metal as the electroplating process continues. Allow the process to continue overnight. If you were successful, you may want to try electroplating your family's dinnerware with silver. Make sure you ask permission first!

Project Idea

Applications of Electrolysis

Electroplating of metals is not the only practical application of electrolysis. In fact, the metals that are used to electro-plate an object are often obtained by electrolysis. For example, copper and aluminum are obtained by the elec-trolysis of certain ores. The process takes weeks and is done on a massive scale. Use the library or search the Internet for information on commercial electrolytic processes. Prepare a report summarizing your findings. Be sure to include information on the energy that is saved by recycling aluminum rather than obtaining it by electrolysis from ores.

Electrolysis has also been used to restore silver coins that have been obtained from sunken treasure. Lying at the bottom of the sea for hundreds of years, these coins became covered with a black coating as a result of the silver's react-ing with chemicals in the ocean. This coating protected the silver underneath. But removing the coating without damaging the coins proved challenging until the use of electrolysis. The chemistry of the events that had been going on beneath the sea and those involved in electrolysis is quite complex. You may want to prepare a report on how electrolysis was used to restore these sunken treasures.

Experiment 2.4

How Can You Turn a Screwdriver into a Magnet?

Materials

* safety goggles
* nonmagnetic screwdriver
* lantern battery (6 volts)
* paper clips
* bare copper wire (20 cm)
* an adult

The word *electromagnetic* suggests that electricity and magnetism are related. In fact, they are related. Both electricity and magnetism are the result of the behavior of electrons. As you have learned, the flow of electrons generates electrical energy. Electrons not only flow but also spin like a top. Electrons are like most people—they prefer not to be alone. Whenever possible, electrons will form pairs. One electron in the pair spins clockwise, while the other electron spins counterclockwise. Their spins neutralize each other. However, if an electron is by itself, its spin will generate a magnetic field. The more unpaired electrons in an atom, the more magnetic the substance.

Iron is classified as a ferromagnetic substance. A **ferromagnetic** substance is magnetic no matter where it is or under what conditions it is exposed. Other substances are paramagnetic. A **paramagnetic** substance may lose its magnetic properties when conditions change. Consider what can happen to a screwdriver by carrying out the following experiment.

Put on a pair of safety goggles to protect your eyes. Wrap a 20-cm piece of copper wire several times around the metal shaft of a nonmagnetic screwdriver, as shown in Figure 15.

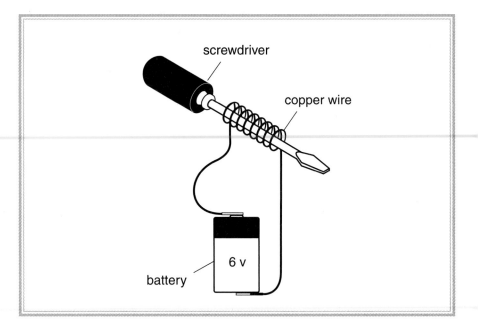

Figure 15. Electrical energy supplied by the battery will magnetize the metal shaft of the screwdriver. The extent to which the screwdriver becomes magnetized depends on the quantity of electrical energy to which it is exposed.

Under adult supervision, briefly touch the bare ends of the wire to the terminals of the battery. Be aware—some sparks will fly! Remove the wire from the screwdriver. Use the screwdriver to pick up paper clips. How long does the screwdriver remain magnetic? Experiment with other small metallic objects in your home to see if you can magnetize them. Be sure to **check with an adult** before you try to magnetize an object.

Project Idea

Electromagnetic Fields

Concerns have been raised about the high-energy fields, known as electromagnetic fields (EMFs), that are produced in the vicinity of high-power transmission lines. Some people feel that exposure to EMFs can cause some types of cancer. Others feel that people are exposed to more EMFs from microwaves and color television sets in their homes than from high-power lines. With the help of an adult, contact your local electrical company to inquire about having a representative visit your home to take EMF measurements. Check the Internet for information about EMFs and possible health hazards.

Chapter 3

Building Supplies

In Chapter 2, you read that batteries operate as a result of one chemical substance losing electrons that another chemical substance gains. Whenever a chemical substance loses electrons, it is said to be oxidized. **Oxidation** is the loss of electrons by a chemical substance. The substance that gains the electrons is said to be reduced. **Reduction** is the gain of electrons by a chemical substance. Oxidation and reduction go hand-in-hand; you cannot have one without the other. Taken together, an oxidation reaction and a reduction reaction are jointly referred to as a **redox reaction**.

Redox reactions occur not only in batteries but also in many other places, including locations in and around your home. For example, a redox reaction is the cause of rust formation on a car or an iron gate. Rust forms when iron becomes oxidized by the oxygen in the air. As the iron is oxidized, it loses electrons to oxygen atoms in the atmosphere. The iron and oxygen react to form a compound called iron oxide, which is commonly known as rust. In addition to iron, other metals can also rust as a result of a redox reaction. Obviously, inhibiting the redox reaction would prevent the formation of rust. To stop rust from forming, metals can be painted or covered with a wax that would serve as a barrier between the metal and the oxygen. The barrier would prevent the transfer of electrons between them.

Another method to prevent rust is to apply a thin layer of another metal in a process known as **galvanization**. The word *galvanization* comes from the name Luigi Galvani, an Italian scientist who studied electricity during the 1700s. In fact, batteries are also known as galvanic cells in his honor.

Experiment 3.1

What Happens When You Soak Galvanized Nails in Vinegar?

Some of the nails sold at a hardware store are galvanized to protect them from rusting. The nails are galvanized by applying a thin layer of zinc metal to cover the iron. Zinc is a more active metal than iron and will give up its electrons more readily to oxygen in the air. As a result, the zinc rusts before the iron can. In effect, the zinc is sacrificed to save the iron. In addition, the compound that forms when zinc and oxygen react serves as a protective barrier for the iron underneath. Here is a simple experiment using galvanized nails to prove that zinc is a more active metal than iron. This experiment is similar to Experiment 1.3, but this time you will collect one of the products made when a metal reacts with an acid.

Place several galvanized nails in an empty plastic pill container. Pour vinegar into the container until it is three-quarters full. Place the cap on the container and invert it. Allow the nails to soak in the vinegar overnight. Look for tiny gas bubbles that form in the vinegar.

The next day, **ask an adult** to light a candle. Over a sink, remove the cap while keeping the pill container inverted.

Allow the nails and vinegar to drain into the sink. Using tongs and wearing an oven mitt, quickly bring the mouth of the container up to the candle flame, as shown in Figure 16. Listen to what happens. Repeat the process, this time using nails that have not been galvanized.

The reaction between the acid in the vinegar and the metal produces hydrogen gas. These are the tiny bubbles that you should have seen forming in the vinegar as the nails soaked. When a flame or spark is introduced, hydrogen gas reacts violently with oxygen gas in the air to produce water. The more violent the reaction, the more hydrogen gas produced. The more hydrogen gas produced, the more the metal has reacted with the acid in the vinegar. Which metal reacted more with the acid—the zinc that coats a galvanized nail or the iron that

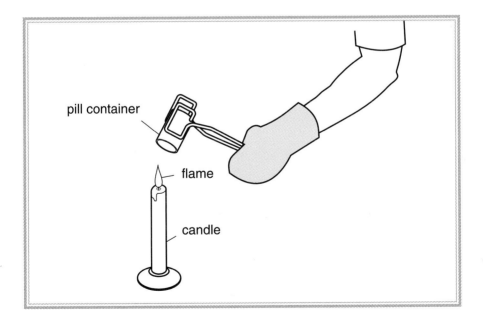

pill container

flame

candle

Figure 16. You should hear a small pop when you hold the empty pill container over a flame. The more galvanized nails you soak in vinegar, the bigger the pop.

is used to make a nongalvanized nail? By the way, can you think of a reason why you had to keep the pill container inverted while you brought it to the flame?

Alloys

Actually, the nongalvanized nails that you used in this experiment are not made entirely of iron. If they were, they would be too soft to hammer. Rather, they are made of steel, which is an alloy. You learned in Chapter 1 that an alloy is a mixture of two or more metals. Nonmetals can also be added to an alloy. For example, the steel used for nails is a 99.8 percent metal alloy (mostly iron) and less than 0.2 percent carbon, which is a nonmetal. That small percentage of carbon gives the alloy the properties needed so that nails can be hammered. Tools such as hammers and screwdrivers are made from high-carbon steel. This steel contains between 0.6 percent and 1.5 percent carbon. The higher the carbon content, the tougher and harder the metal.

Steel is not the only alloy that has been put to practical use. Another is brass, an alloy used to make screws and various hardware items such as hinges and doorknobs. Brass contains the metals copper, zinc, tin, lead, and manganese. Still another alloy is based on the metal titanium. Titanium alloys are quite strong. Over ten thousand pounds of titanium alloys are used to build each engine in a 747 jet airplane. In contrast, the amount of zinc used to produce a galvanized layer is quite small.

The Galvanized Layer

The layer of zinc metal that is used to galvanize an object such as a nail is very thin. You can actually determine the thickness of the zinc layer based on the density of the metal. **Density** is the ratio of mass to volume. Mass is simply how much "stuff" there is. Volume is the amount of space the "stuff" occupies. Density is a measure of how tightly matter is packed. Which of the objects shown in Figure 17 is more dense?

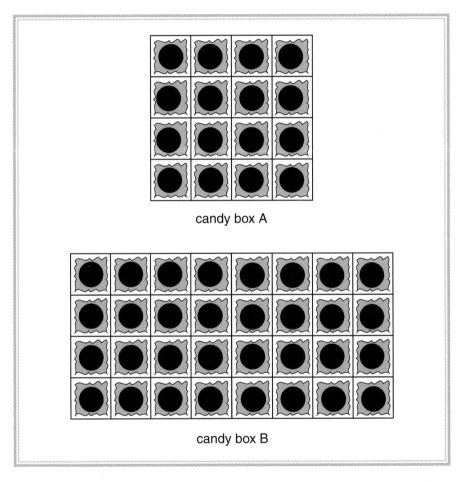

candy box A

candy box B

Figure 17. Because density is a ratio, you must consider both the mass and volume of an object. The candy box on the bottom has twice the volume of the other but also contains twice as many candies. As a result, both these boxes have the same mass-to-volume ratio. Thus both candy boxes have the same density.

Perhaps you have heard the phrase "you're really dense." Usually this is a negative comment that is applied to someone who does not seem to be thinking too clearly. But if you know what density is, the phrase could apply to someone who is thinking quite clearly. Actually, telling someone that they are "really dense" could imply that there is a lot of brain mass occupying that person's skull.

Experiment 3.2

How Thick Is the Galvanized Layer on Metal?

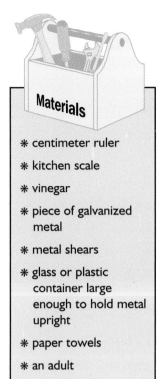

Materials

- ✳ centimeter ruler
- ✳ kitchen scale
- ✳ vinegar
- ✳ piece of galvanized metal
- ✳ metal shears
- ✳ glass or plastic container large enough to hold metal upright
- ✳ paper towels
- ✳ an adult

Density is usually expressed in units of grams per milliliter, or g/mL. Another way of expressing density is in units of grams per cubic centimeter, or g/cm^3. The density of zinc is 7.14 g/cm^3. With the use of this value, you can actually determine the thickness of the zinc layer on a galvanized object. In this experiment, you may want to have your science teacher check the calculations that are required in the results.

If you cannot find any galvanized metal at home, ask at a hardware store or a junkyard for a scrap piece. **Ask an adult** to use metal shears to cut the piece of metal into the shape of a rectangle so that it can fit upright into a glass or plastic container. Use a kitchen scale to determine the mass of the metal. Record the mass of the metal in grams. If your kitchen scale is not calibrated in grams, then use the following conversion:

1 ounce = 28 grams

Measure the length and width of the metal in centimeters (cm). Place the metal in the container and cover it with vinegar. Allow the metal to remain in the vinegar until all the zinc that forms the coating has reacted with the acid. You can tell when the reaction is complete when no more hydrogen gas bubbles are formed. To be sure that all the zinc has reacted, replace the vinegar with a fresh supply. If no gas bubbles form after the vinegar has been replenished, then all the zinc has reacted.

Pour the used vinegar down a drain. Remove the metal, rinse it thoroughly with running water, and dry it with paper towels. Reweigh the metal. The metal should weigh less because the zinc has been removed. Calculate the mass of the zinc used to coat the metal. Do this by subtracting the mass of the metal after it was placed in the vinegar from the mass of the metal before it was placed in the vinegar.

Calculate the area of the metal rectangle by multiplying the length by the width. Because the zinc metal coats both sides, the area covered by the zinc is twice the area of the galvanized metal. Your answer should be expressed in square centimeters (cm^2).

Next, calculate the volume of zinc on the metal. To do this, multiply the mass of the zinc by the inverse of the density of the zinc. The mass units (g) will cancel, leaving the volume unit (cm^3).

$$\text{g zinc} \quad \times \quad \frac{1 \text{ cm}^3}{7.14 \text{ g}} \quad = \quad \text{cm}^3 \text{ (volume covered by zinc)}$$

Next, divide the volume of zinc on the metal (cm^3) by the area of the metal rectangle (cm^2).

$$\frac{\text{volume zinc (cm}^3)}{\text{area zinc (cm}^2)} \quad = \quad \text{thickness of zinc (cm)}$$

For an added challenge, calculate the thickness of the zinc coating in terms of the number of zinc atoms that form the coat. The radius of a zinc atom is 2.66 x 10^{-8} cm.

Metric System

In this experiment, you were required to record your measurements and perform your calculation using centimeters (cm) and grams (g). These units are part of the metric system. The metric system is one that is based on tens. As a result, conversions between units are easy to perform, unlike the system used in the United States. Just consider what you have to do when converting gallons to fluid ounces. You first have to multiply the number of gallons by 4 to convert to quarts. Then you have to multiply this value by 32 to convert to fluid ounces. Thus, 1.2 gallons = 4.8 quarts = 153.6 fluid ounces.

Now consider what you do when converting volume units in the metric system. To convert liters to centiliters, you multiply by 100 or move the decimal point two places to the right. To convert centiliters to milliliters, you multiply by 10 or move the decimal point one place to the right. Thus, 1.2 liters = 120 centiliters = 1,200 milliliters. You can see that you do not need a calculator to perform conversions in the metric system once you recognize what the prefixes mean. Table 1 lists the common prefixes used in the metric system. How many grams are equal to 75.68 milligrams?

Now you recognize the advantage of the metric system: the ease of converting between units. Keep in mind that the metric system is not more accurate than any other system of measurements, including the one used in the United States. You can measure the length of your room just as accurately in

Table 1. Metric Prefixes

Prefix	Units	Symbol	Meaning
giga	10^9	G	billion
mega	10^6	M	million
kilo	10^3	k	thousand
deci	10^{-1}	d	tenth
centi	10^{-2}	c	hundredth
milli	10^{-3}	m	thousandth
micro	10^{-6}	μ	millionth
nano	10^{-9}	n	billionth

yards as you can in meters. However, converting the value in yards to inches is more involved mathematically than converting the value in meters to centimeters.

Scientists throughout the world use the metric system for their measurements in the laboratory. In 1960, the scientific community adopted a subset of the metric system to use as the standard scientific system of measurement units. This is the "Système Internationale d'Unités," or SI for short. The SI system includes seven base units that are listed in Table 2. Any SI unit can be modified with prefixes to match the scale of the object being measured. While meters may be suitable to measure a person's height, micrometers (10^{-6} m) are more appropriate for measuring the size of cells.

The seven SI base units cannot measure every observable property. Thus, derived units are created by either multiplying or dividing the seven base units in various ways. For example, in the previous experiment, the volume of zinc on

Table 2. SI Base Units

Quantity	Unit	Symbol
length	meter	m
mass	kilogram	kg
time	second	s
temperature	kelvin	K
amount	mole	mol
electric current	ampere	A
luminous intensity	candela	cd

the metal was expressed in cm^3 (cm x cm x cm). The area covered by the zinc was expressed in cm^2 (cm x cm). If you had to measure the speed of an object, you would divide the distance traveled, using the base unit meter (m), by the time it took, using the base unit second (s). Thus, speed could be expressed as m/s, which can then be converted to km/hour.

Experiment 3.3

What Is the Densest Object You Can Find?

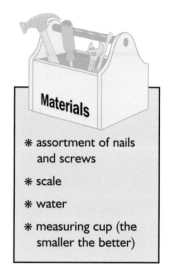

Materials

* assortment of nails and screws
* scale
* water
* measuring cup (the smaller the better)

You probably use the metric system when you carry out a science experiment in school. For example, you may have measured the volume of a liquid in milliliters or the mass of an object in grams. But chances are that your science classroom is the only place you have used the metric system. The following experiment will provide you with an opportunity to practice using the metric system at home. You will determine which is the densest nail or screw that you can find at your hardware store.

Be sure to get an assortment of different types of nails and screws, including those made of both galvanized and nongalvanized metals and brass. Check with an employee at a hardware store if you are not sure what metals are present in the different nails and screws that you find.

Earlier in this chapter, you read that density is usually expressed in the units g/mL. These are the units you will use to calculate the density of each type of nail and screw. But first you must learn how to measure volumes using the water displacement method. Simply pour some water into a measuring cup marked in milliliters (mL). Record the volume of water you added. You will find it convenient to add the water up to one of the lines marked on the cup, for example the 100 mL mark.

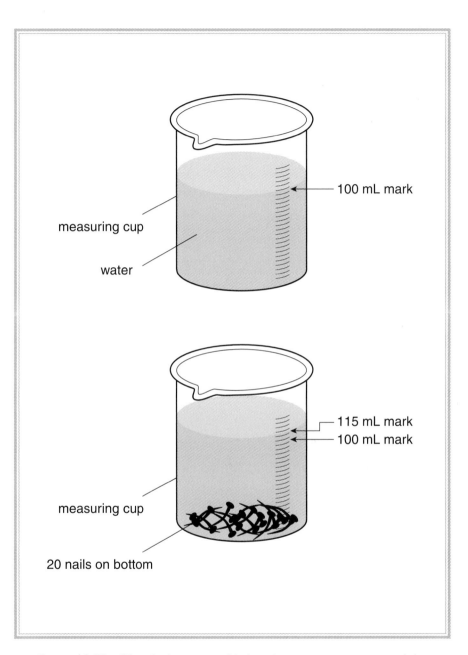

measuring cup

water

100 mL mark

115 mL mark
100 mL mark

measuring cup

20 nails on bottom

Figure 18. The 20 nails that were added to this measuring cup caused the volume to increase from 100 mL to 115 mL. Thus 20 nails were responsible for an increase in volume of 15 mL. Each nail therefore occupies a volume of 15 mL/20 nails = 0.75 mL/nail.

Next drop in one nail or screw and see how much the volume increases. This represents the volume occupied by that object.

One nail or screw most likely did not cause a noticeable increase in the volume, especially if you used a large measuring cup. In that case, drop in ten, twenty, or as many identical nails or screws as necessary until you can measure an increase in volume. Make sure that all the objects you drop in are made of the same metal or alloy and are the same size. To determine the volume of just one of the objects, divide the volume increase by the number of objects you placed in the measuring cup. For example, the volume occupied by one nail in Figure 18 is 0.75 mL.

Once you know the volume of the object, determine its mass by placing it on a scale. If one nail or screw does not register a noticeable increase in mass, then place ten or twenty of them on the scale. Again be sure to divide the total increase in mass by the number of objects you weighed to get the mass of just one object. Now divide the mass of the object by the volume you obtained earlier to calculate the density of that object. Prepare a table listing the densities of each type of nail and screw you measured.

None of the densities you calculated will even come close to that of osmium, a blue-white metal. With a density of 22.6 g/mL, osmium is the densest substance on Earth. It is so dense that a piece of osmium the size of a football would be too heavy for you to lift. If you can calculate the volume of a football, then you should be able to determine how much this sample of osmium would weigh. Simply multiply the volume (mL) of the football by its density (g/mL). Notice that the volume units (mL) cancel, leaving the mass unit (g).

Project Idea

The Status of the Metric System in the United States

Along with Myanmar and Liberia, the United States is one of only three nonmetric countries in the world. In the United States, gasoline is sold in gallons, not liters; meat is sold by the pound, not kilograms; and distance is measured in miles, not kilometers. Sporadic attempts have been made in the past to convert to the metric system. For example, you may see baseball fields marked in meters in addition to feet. However, a full and complete conversion has never been achieved.

Pressure on the United States to convert to the metric system has been mounting. In 1988, Congress passed a law that requires government agencies and their customers to use metrics. Beginning in the year 2000, countries belonging to the European Community will no longer allow the import of nonmetric equipment.

Carry out a project to convert anything that is currently measured in nonmetric units in your house to metric units. Begin with yourself. For example, if you weigh 100 pounds (lb), then your weight in the metric system is 45.4 kilograms (kg). See how many items now measured in nonmetric units would have to be converted. Then do the same for everything nonmetric that you encounter on a daily basis outside your house. For example, the distance you travel to school would be 5.6 kilometers (km) rather than 3.5 miles (m). Prepare a table listing all the conversions that you discovered you had to do. Once you complete your table, you will appreciate what will be involved in converting the United States to a metric system.

Experiment 3.4

The Simple Machine Challenge

Materials

* ruler
* pencil
* 2 quarters
* empty soda can
* string
* hammer
* safety goggles
* nail
* bucket
* water

Simple machines are devices that are designed to perform some kind of work with only one movement. There are six simple machines: the lever, the inclined plane, the wedge, the screw, the pulley, and the wheel and axle. You can find examples of these simple machines in a hardware store. Many of them are located in the building supply section.

A lever is a bar that is free to pivot about a fixed point. Levers that you could find in a hardware store include a crowbar, which can be useful in dismantling an old building, and a hammer, which can be used to remove nails. An inclined plane is a slanted surface used to raise an object. Builders use ramps to move supplies during construction. The objects must be moved over a longer distance, but much less effort is needed than if they were to be lifted straight up. A wedge is an inclined plane that moves. Both a knife and an axe are examples of wedges. A screw is an inclined plane wrapped around a cylinder to form a spiral. In addition, a C-clamp, such as the one shown in Figure 19, is an example of how a screw can be used to hold things together. A pulley is a chain, belt, or rope wrapped around a wheel. Pulleys are often used for clotheslines. A wheel and axle is a lever that rotates in a circle around

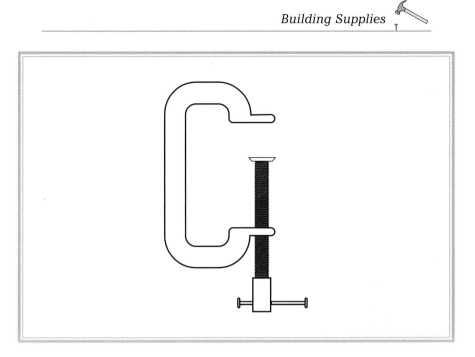

Figure 19. As the screw turns, the clamp tightens. By the way, this C-clamp consists of two simple tools. One is the screw. What is the other?

an axle. Examples of this type of simple tool you might find in a hardware store include bicycle wheels and gears.

Now that you know what the six simple machines are, here is your chance to see if you can put some of these devices to use. Your challenge will be to modify some simple tools to see what works best.

Place a ruler (lever) on a pencil, as shown in Figure 20a. See how far you can propel a quarter that is placed on the ruler by dropping another quarter onto the ruler. Experiment with factors that you can vary. For example, position the pencil at different spots under the ruler and drop the quarter from different heights.

Wearing safety goggles, use a hammer and nail to poke some holes along the side of an empty soda can, as shown in

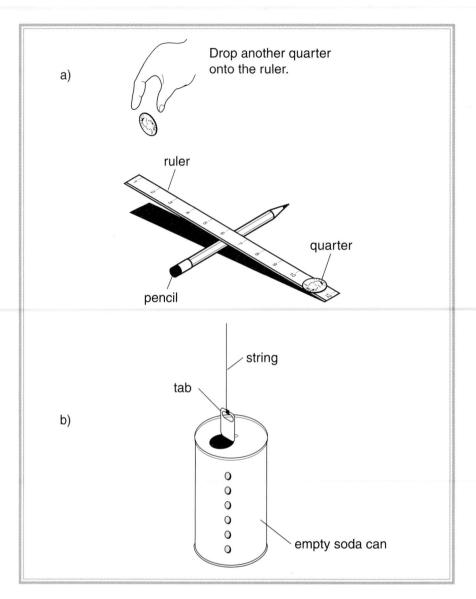

Figure 20. a) When placed over a pencil as shown, a ruler serves as a lever that can propel objects, such as a quarter, through the air. b) The soda can with holes will spin like a wheel as water pours out from the holes punched down the side. The holes must be made so that they point at an angle and not straight out from the can. A string acts as an axle by suspending the can (wheel). Together the can (wheel) and the string (axle) mimic the action of a sprinkler.

Figure 20b. Be sure that all the holes point at an angle and in the same direction. Use string to suspend the can by the tab. Lower the can into a bucket of water that you have set up outdoors. Be prepared to get wet. Slowly lift the can out of the water and observe how a sprinkler (wheel and axle) works. Experiment to see how far you can make the water squirt out of the can. Vary the number of holes in the can and the distance between the holes. Check to see if the size of the can affects how well your sprinkler works.

What other simple machines can you identify throughout your home and the hardware store? Perhaps you can think of a way to improve an existing tool. Your school may have an invention contest in which you can enter your improved tool.

Chapter 4

Plumbing Supplies

Whether you are drinking water from your kitchen faucet at home or from a water fountain at your school, the water you are drinking is not 100 percent pure water. Water from a faucet contains many dissolved materials, including salts, minerals, gases, and natural pollutants such as decayed animal and plant matter. In addition, chemicals are often added to water for health reasons. For example, you may live in an area where small quantities of fluoride are placed in the drinking water to help prevent tooth decay. Chlorine gas is also usually added to water before it is pumped from reservoirs into homes. Because it is poisonous, the chlorine kills any harmful bacteria present in the drinking water. However, the amount of chlorine added is too small to cause any harm to humans.

If your drinking water comes from a well, you may have experienced an unpleasant taste at times. This is caused by a high level of salts and minerals that can seep into the underground water supply. As the water seeps through the ground, it picks up these chemical substances. Whenever these salts and minerals are present in high levels, the water is said to be hard. If the levels are low, the water is said to be soft. One characteristic of hard water is its inability to form suds when soap is used. Hard water may also clog drains and pipes because the minerals and salts gradually form deposits that can block the flow of water.

Experiment 4.1

How Can You Make Soft Water?

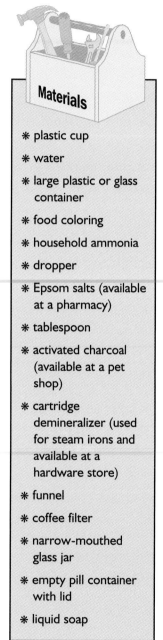

Materials

* plastic cup
* water
* large plastic or glass container
* food coloring
* household ammonia
* dropper
* Epsom salts (available at a pharmacy)
* tablespoon
* activated charcoal (available at a pet shop)
* cartridge demineralizer (used for steam irons and available at a hardware store)
* funnel
* coffee filter
* narrow-mouthed glass jar
* empty pill container with lid
* liquid soap

Before reaching homes in a community that receives its water from reservoirs, the water is sometimes treated to reduce its hardness. The water is passed through filters containing chemicals that trap the salts and minerals, making the water soft. In wells or community systems where the water is hard, commercially available softeners can be installed to soften the water. Because they contain chemicals that remove minerals from the water, these softeners are known as *demineralizers*. These demineralizers may also contain activated charcoal to remove some of the dissolved gases and colored chemicals that can give water an unpleasant appearance, odor, or taste. You probably can find such a demineralizer in the plumbing supply section of your hardware store. Or you can make your own water softener.

To prepare hard water, begin by almost filling a plastic cup with water. Add food coloring drop by drop, while stirring, until a pale color is visible. Add some household ammonia drop by drop, while stirring, until the water has a faint odor of ammonia. Pour one tablespoon of Epsom salts into the water and stir until dissolved.

Empty the contents of a small cartridge demineralizer into a plastic or glass container. Add an equal amount of activated charcoal and thoroughly mix the two. Set up a filter apparatus as shown in Figure 21. Place the demineralizer-charcoal mixture in a filter-paper-lined funnel. Filter approximately half of the water sample you prepared through this apparatus. Collect the liquid that passes through the filter in a clean container such as a narrow-mouthed glass jar. The liquid that collects in the jar is called a **filtrate**. If the filtrate is still

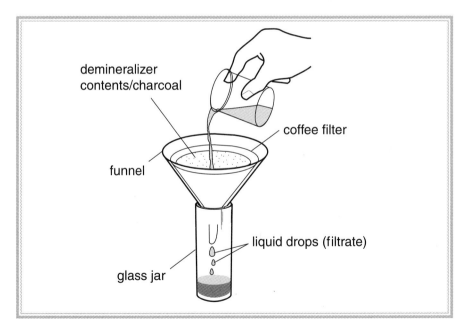

Figure 21. Filter the water slowly so that it does not spill over the filter paper and pass directly into the jar. If this happens, some of the water will not be filtered before it collects in the jar. If you do not have a narrow-mouthed glass jar, you can use a tall drinking glass to collect your filter water.

colored or has an odor, keep passing the water back through the filter until the water is both colorless and odorless.

To test the softness of the filtrate, fill an empty pill container halfway with the filtered water sample. Add three to four drops of liquid soap to the filtrate, replace the cap, and shake vigorously for one minute. Repeat this process, this time using the water sample that was not filtered.

Compare how many soapsuds were formed with both water samples. Epsom salts contain a chemical called magnesium sulfate, which makes the water hard. The food coloring colors the water, and the ammonia gives it an odor. If your water softener worked well, then the filtrate should have produced more suds and should have been colorless and odorless. If you have a demineralizer at home, test the water that comes out of the faucet for its softness. Why are demineralizers sold for steam irons?

Project Idea

Checking Water for Bacteria

Water treatment processes do not kill all the living things in water before it reaches homes. Design an experiment to determine the different kinds of bacteria that still remain in water as it comes out of the faucet in your home. You will need to learn techniques in **microbiology**, which is the study of small organisms such as bacteria and viruses. You can ask your science teacher for help in setting up and carrying out your project.

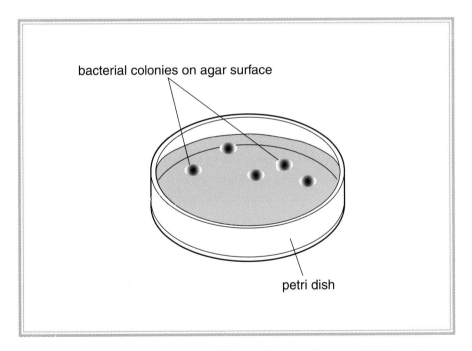

bacterial colonies on agar surface

petri dish

Figure 22. The agar in the petri dish provides a surface on which bacteria can grow. Nutrients in the agar enable the bacteria to grow and divide. One bacterial cell is too small to see with your eyes. However, if one is placed on the agar, it can divide to produce a colony that you can easily see. Each colony is made of millions of bacterial cells, which all came from that one bacterial cell.

You must first learn how to prepare a sterile environment in which to grow bacteria. Small round containers known as *petri dishes* are used for this purpose. A substance called agar is added to a petri dish to serve as a solid surface on which bacteria can grow. Nutrients are added to the agar to supply the bacteria with what they need to grow and multiply. Sterile petri dishes already prepared with agar and the appropriate nutrients can be obtained from a scientific supply company. All you have to do is use a sterile applicator to apply a sample of water to the surface of the agar. The petri dish is then left undisturbed for several days, either at room temperature or in a temperature-controlled incubator. Any bacteria present in the water sample will develop into colonies that are easily visible, as you can see in Figure 22.

If you decide to carry out this project, be sure to work under adult supervision. Never come in contact with the bacteria, as they may be ones that cause disease. Be sure to dispose of all petri dishes that contain any bacteria in a proper manner. One way is to soak the dishes in bleach overnight to kill the bacteria. Then rinse the dishes thoroughly with running tap water before disposing of them.

Experiment 4.2

How Can You Make 100 Percent Pure Water?

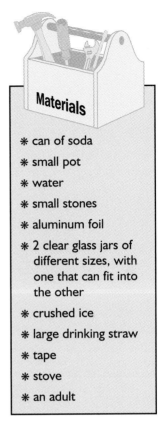

Materials

* ✳ can of soda
* ✳ small pot
* ✳ water
* ✳ small stones
* ✳ aluminum foil
* ✳ 2 clear glass jars of different sizes, with one that can fit into the other
* ✳ crushed ice
* ✳ large drinking straw
* ✳ tape
* ✳ stove
* ✳ an adult

A water filter that you can buy in the plumbing section of a hardware store will not remove all of the salts, minerals, and other substances present in water. These filters mainly remove small particles and some of the salts and minerals that make water hard. The salts are present in water as ions. You learned in Chapter 2 that an ion is a charged particle that is formed when an atom either loses or gains an electron. As water passes through a demineralizer, some ions are removed. The water that passes through is known as **deionized water**. But even deionized water is not 100 percent pure water, as it still contains some ions in addition to other substances.

To get pure water, you must distill, not deionize, it. In Chapter 1, you learned that distilled water is 100 percent pure water. You also read that distilled water can be made in the laboratory or purchased in a hardware store. The process used to make distilled water is known as **distillation**. If your school has the necessary apparatus, you may have made some distilled water to use when testing the pH of your soil samples.

But if you were not able to make any, here is your chance to carry out a distillation using a disposable apparatus. This procedure will not give you enough distilled water to use in an experiment, but at least you will know how it is made.

Open a can of soda and take a drink until the can is no more than half full. Place the soda can in a small pot. Add some water to the pot, making sure that the soda can does not tip over. You can place some small stones in the can to keep it upright. Place a smaller glass jar inside a larger one. Surround the smaller jar with crushed ice. Place both jars on a countertop near the stove. Make sure that the level of the pot on the stove is higher than the level of the glass jars on the countertop.

Wrap a sheet of aluminum foil several times around a large drinking straw. Use tape to make sure that the aluminum foil does not unravel when you slide it off the straw. Slide the aluminum tube off the straw. Place one end of the tube into the can so that it rests above the level of the soda. Bend the aluminum tube and place the other end into the smaller glass jar as shown in Figure 23.

Under the supervision of an adult, gently heat the soda can by turning on the burner. Make sure that the pot always contains some water. Observe what collects in the small jar. As the soda boils, some of the vapor makes its way through the aluminum tube. Air surrounding the tube causes the vapor to turn back into a liquid that collects in this small jar. The liquid that collects in the jar is distilled water. If you do not get any distilled water, make sure that not all the vapor formed inside the can escapes into the air. Check for leaks in the aluminum tube. Use foil and tape to seal any leaks. But

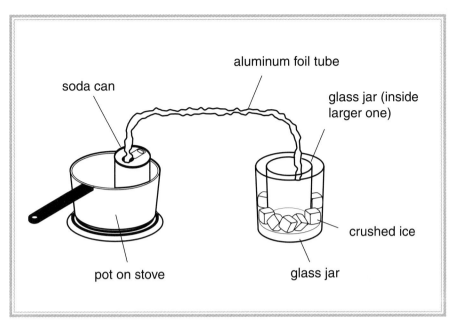

Figure 23. Water vapor formed inside the can as the soda is heated is cooled by the air as it travels through the aluminum tube. The liquid then collects in the jar. What might happen if the water vapor were kept trapped inside the soda can?

be sure that you do not completely seal the can or pinch the aluminum tube so that it is constricted. The vapor must not be allowed to build up inside the can where it may cause the can to explode. Taste the distilled water after it has cooled. How does it taste compared with the soda?

Fractional Distillation

A variation of the distillation technique you just performed is known as fractional distillation. **Fractional distillation** is a process that separates the components of a mixture based on their boiling points. This process is used to separate the various components in petroleum—that thick, dark-brown liquid that supplies much of the world's energy. Petroleum is used to make a variety of consumer products, including plastics, and many of the top twenty-five chemicals produced in the United States. In turn, these chemicals are used to make other products, including many that are found in a hardware store. Obviously, petroleum is a valuable commodity that contains thousands of different compounds that have become part of our daily lives.

All the different compounds in petroleum have one thing in common. They are all hydrocarbons. A **hydrocarbon** is an organic compound that is made entirely of just two kinds of atoms—carbon and hydrogen. Before petroleum can be made useful, the various hydrocarbons must be separated in the refinery by fractional distillation. This process depends on the differences in the boiling points of the various liquid hydrocarbons present in petroleum. As the petroleum is heated, the liquid with the lowest boiling point will vaporize into a gas first. Cooling this gas causes it to form into a liquid again so that it can be collected and isolated from those hydrocarbons that have not reached their boiling point. As the temperature is increased, hydrocarbons with successively higher boiling points are vaporized, cooled, and collected. Figure 24 shows some of the products that are isolated from petroleum by fractional distillation.

Clogged Pipes

The water that comes out of your faucet may be filtered to make it cleaner and softer, but it certainly is not clean and soft when it goes down the drain. In fact, the water may be so full of dirt and grease that it clogs the pipes. Either a wire "snake"

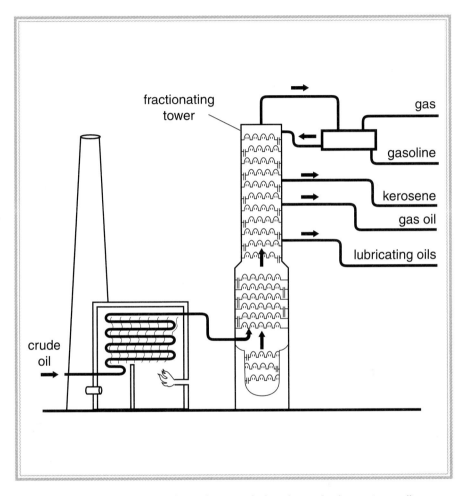

Figure 24. The lightest hydrocarbons with their lower boiling points collect at the top. Which hydrocarbons are these? The heaviest ones with their higher boiling points collect at the bottom. Which ones are these?

or a chemical drain cleaner will have to be used to unclog the pipe. You can find both these plumbing products in a hardware store. The snake is simply forced down the drain, pushing out whatever is clogging the pipe. But how does a drain cleaner work? A chemical in the drain cleaner reacts with the grease in the clogged pipe to make soap. The soap can then wash away whatever remains, and the pipe is no longer clogged. Making soap is known as saponification. The process of saponification goes back hundreds of years.

Experiment 4.3

Can Fat Really Become Soap?

The early Romans mixed the ashes from burned wood with the fat from sacrificed animals to form a crude soap. In Europe during the Middle Ages, soap was prepared by combining the ashes from burned wood with the fat from goats. With the development of chemistry as a science in the eighteenth century, scientists discovered simpler, cleaner, and cheaper ways to make soap. But all these processes use the same two basic ingredients, as you will find out in this experiment.

Put on a pair of protective eye goggles and rubber gloves and ask an adult to do the same. **Ask the adult** to mix 16 ounces of lard with 2 ounces of drain cleaner in a pot. Be very careful when adding the drain cleaner because the chemical it contains can cause serious skin burns. If any does spill on your skin, rinse it off thoroughly in running water. Add 4 fluid ounces of rubbing alcohol to the pot.

Ask the adult to gently heat the mixture while stirring. Bring the mixture almost to a boil. Be very careful not to splatter any of the mixture on the stove because alcohol is flammable. Add 2 fluid ounces of water and stir thoroughly. While the mixture is cooling, dissolve one tablespoon of table salt in 4 fluid ounces of water. Pour the cooled mixture of lard and drain cleaner into the salt solution. After allowing the contents to cool completely, remove the solid that forms. This is soap.

The lye in the drain cleaner is a base called sodium hydroxide. You learned in Chapter 1 that a base is a chemical that produces a solution with a pH greater than 7. Sodium hydroxide is a strong base as indicated by the fact that liquid drain cleaners have a pH value of 11. The sodium hydroxide in the drain cleaner reacts with the fat in the lard to produce soap. You want to make sure that all the sodium hydroxide has reacted so that your soap is not basic, or it will irritate the skin. You can check the pH of the soap you made to make sure that its pH value is less than 8. Refer to Experiment 1.2 for information on how to test the pH of a solution. If the soap is too basic, place it in the pot again and heat it until it liquefies. Continue heating for fifteen minutes so that any sodium hydroxide present will react with the fat. You can also add more lard to the soap.

Project Idea

Making Different Kinds of Soap

Lard is only one type of fat to use in making soap. Other animal fats that can be used include goat fat, lanolin, mutton fat, and tallow. Vegetable fats can also be used. These include canola, castor, coconut, corn, olive, palm, peanut, and safflower oils. **Under adult supervision**, carry out a project to see what kinds of soaps you can make using these fats and oils. Use a small amount of perfume or aftershave lotion to scent your soaps. Devise some method to evaluate the various soaps you make. You will want to test how well they remove dirt from your skin and clothes.

Experiment 4.4

How Well Do Detergents Work?

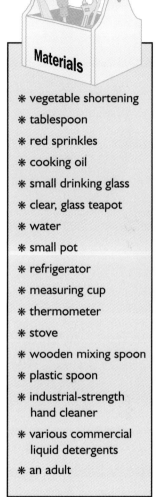

Materials

* vegetable shortening
* tablespoon
* red sprinkles
* cooking oil
* small drinking glass
* clear, glass teapot
* water
* small pot
* refrigerator
* measuring cup
* thermometer
* stove
* wooden mixing spoon
* plastic spoon
* industrial-strength hand cleaner
* various commercial liquid detergents
* an adult

Chemicals in soaps react with minerals and salts in hard water to produce a solid substance that does not easily dissolve in water. A familiar example of this solid substance is the ring left in a bathtub after bathing. Recognizing that this residue might pose a problem in households where the water is naturally hard, chemists sought for ways to prevent the formation of this solid substance without reducing the cleansing power of soap. They came up with detergents.

Both soaps and detergents work by dispersing the oils and grease in water. These oils and grease bind dirt. By dispersing the oils and grease in water, the dirt is no longer trapped and thus can be washed away. This process is known as emulsifying. **Emulsifying** simply means that the detergent can break up the grease and oils into very small droplets that can then mix with water. Figure 25 shows how soaps and detergents emulsify oils and grease. The better a detergent emulsifies, the more effective it is in getting out dirt. This experiment will show you how to test

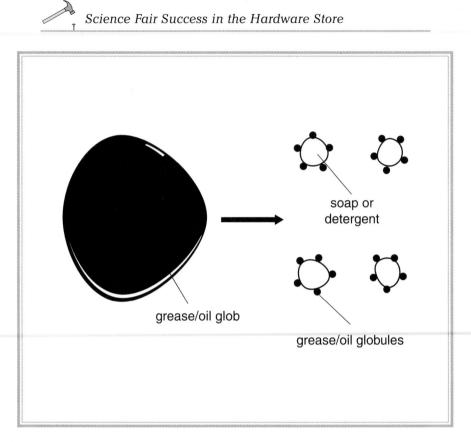

Figure 25. Normally, grease particles and water do not mix. However, each soap or detergent particle can break down, or emulsify, grease or oil globs into much smaller globules. In this way, the grease or oil becomes suspended in water and can then be washed away. Any dirt trapped in the grease or oil is also washed away.

the effectiveness of an industrial-strength hand cleaner. Such hand cleaners are sold by hardware stores for use by plumbers and others who often get their hands greasy and dirty at work.

To observe the emulsifying process more easily, first prepare a grease sample by adding a few drops of red food coloring to vegetable shortening. Be sure to stir thoroughly to mix the two. The coloring will enable you to observe what happens to the grease as it is mixed with water and the detergent.

Pour 2 cups of water in a clear, glass teapot. **Under adult supervision**, heat the water on a stove until its temperature reaches 100°F. Adjust the burner on the stove so that the water temperature remains as close as possible to this temperature throughout the experiment. This is about the temperature used for washing clothes with a detergent.

Add one tablespoon of the colored grease sample to the warm water. Use the handle of a wooden mixing spoon to mix the water and colored grease sample. Notice that the grease sample does not mix with the water but remains as a distinct glob on the surface, as shown in Figure 26a. Use a plastic spoon to add a small amount of an industrial-strength hand cleaner to the water-grease mixture. Again swirl the water with a wooden spoon and observe what happens to the grease sample. Continue adding the detergent until the grease sample is completely emulsified. You can tell this point is reached when all the grease sample has been emulsified into tiny globules that are dispersed throughout the water, as shown in Figure 26b.

You can use this procedure to test the relative effectiveness of commercial liquid detergents that are used to wash clothes. Rather than buying several different brands, check with your friends to see which ones they use. You can invite them to participate in your experiment by asking them to bring their detergent to test. For each brand that you test, set up the water and colored grease mixture. Then slowly add the liquid detergent until the grease sample is completely dispersed. You will need to know the volume of detergent that must be added to

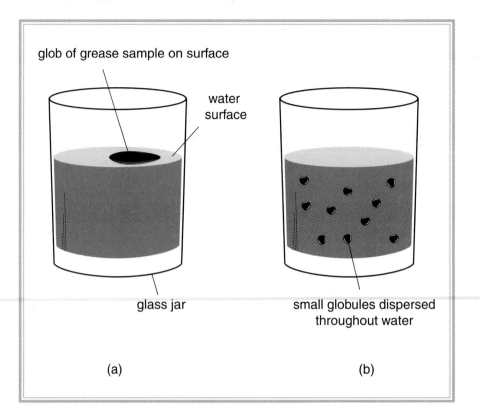

glob of grease sample on surface

water surface

glass jar

small globules dispersed throughout water

(a)   (b)

Figure 26. a) When added to water, the lard will remain as a distinct glob on the surface. b) You can tell that the detergent has emulsified all the lard when all the lard has become dispersed as very small globules throughout the water. If left standing, the small globules may form a thin layer that covers the entire surface of the warm water.

disperse all the grease sample. Simply record the volume of the detergent in the measuring cup both at the start and end of your experiment. The difference represents the volume you used to disperse all the grease sample. The less detergent used, the more effective it is in emulsifying oils and grease.

Experiment 4.5

What Properties Do Metals Share?

Materials

* short piece of copper pipe
* brass screw
* steel washer
* metal file
* 3 small glass jars
* water
* mineral spirits
* table salt
* candle wax
* old baking sheet
* oven
* an adult

The drains that get clogged are sometimes made of metal, especially those found in older houses. If you look among the plumbing supplies at a hardware store, you will notice a variety of items made from metals. You might find copper pipes, brass faucets, and steel washers. Metals are usually shiny, or, as chemists say, have a luster. But there are substances that are shiny that are not metals. Silicon, for example, has a metallic sheen but is not a metal. Silicon is a substance that is used to make computer chips. On the other hand, there are metals that have a dull appearance. Is there one property then that sets metals apart from all other substances?

The one characteristic property of all metals is their ability to conduct electricity. Even the poorest conductive metal conducts electricity one hundred times better than the best conductive nonmetal. Copper is an excellent conductor of electricity. That is why copper metal is used for electrical wiring. But what makes metals suitable for use in plumbing supplies? This experiment will show you why certain metals are used in plumbing.

Use the metal file to get shavings of copper, brass, and stainless steel, as shown in Figure 27. Place the shavings in three glass jars, with one metal in each jar. Label each jar. Add water to see if any of the metals dissolve.

Pour off the water from each jar. **Under adult supervision,** pour some mineral spirits into each jar. Perform this step outdoors or in a well-ventilated area so that the fumes from the mineral spirits can quickly dissipate. Observe which metal, if any, dissolves. Pour off the mineral spirits into a jar for proper disposal. Dispose of any metal shavings that remain.

Place some table salt and candle wax into two separate glass jars. Both solid table salt and wax are nonconductors. Check to see if they dissolve in water. Repeat this process, this time checking to see if they dissolve in mineral spirits.

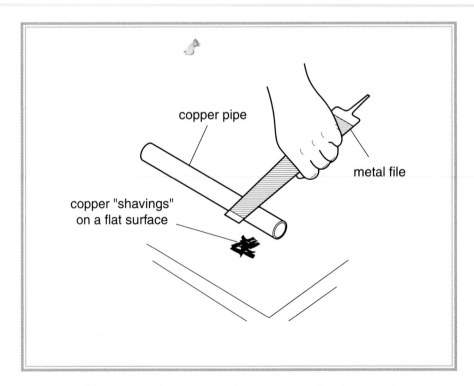

copper pipe

metal file

copper "shavings" on a flat surface

Figure 27. Carefully file a piece of metal to get the shavings that you will need.

Place some fresh metal shavings and pea-sized samples of table salt and wax on a metal baking sheet. Keep each item separate. Place the sheet in the oven. Turn on the oven to 200 degrees. Observe the sequence in which the substances melt as you slowly increase the heat.

Metals do not readily dissolve or melt. Chemists simply say that metals generally are insoluble and have high melting points. Why do these properties make metals suitable for use in plumbing?

Project Idea

Chemical Bonds

Atoms are held together by a force of attraction known as a chemical bond. The chemical bond that holds the atoms in a metal together are logically called *metallic bonds*. Those that hold the ions together in table salt are called *ionic bonds*. The bonds that hold together the atoms that make up wax are called *covalent bonds*. To get your project started, research these different types of bonds. Include a model of each type of chemical bond as part of your project. The metallic bonds in metals are responsible for many of their properties, including their ability to conduct electricity. Your report can include information on how and why metals conduct electricity better than other substances. This property has something to do with conduction bands, which may be included as part of your models of chemical bonds.

Chapter 5

Recreational Supplies

Your family has gathered for a barbecue when, suddenly, dark, rain-threatening clouds begin to appear and cover what was once a perfectly clear, blue sky. As soon as everyone sits down to enjoy those delicious-looking grilled hamburgers and hot dogs, the rain starts. While rushing to get the food inside before everything gets soaked, someone suggests that the next time a barbecue is planned, the family should check for an updated weather report. Someone volunteers to listen to the all-weather channel on television. Someone else will tune in the all-weather station on the radio. Still another person will go on the Internet to check the local forecast. But you can volunteer to inform your family about the chances of rain without looking at the television, listening to the radio, or checking the Internet. One way is to use a barometer. With the help of a barometer, you can forecast the weather to help plan your family's outdoor recreational activities.

Experiment 5.1

How Does a Barometer Forecast the Weather?

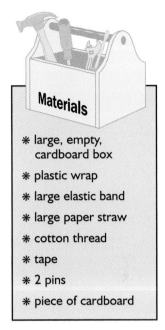

Materials

* large, empty, cardboard box
* plastic wrap
* large elastic band
* large paper straw
* cotton thread
* tape
* 2 pins
* piece of cardboard

A barometer depends on changes in atmospheric pressure. Whenever a weather report is given, the barometric pressure is usually included. **Barometric pressure** is the pressure exerted by the atmosphere, or the air around you, that causes a column of mercury inside a barometer to rise or fall. Barometric pressure is usually reported in the United States in a nonmetric unit—inches. The inches represent the height to which a column of mercury will rise depending on the barometric pressure. The higher the atmospheric pressure, the higher the column.

A rising barometer is an indication that the weather will be favorable because high pressure is associated with clear skies. On the other hand, a falling barometer indicates that inclement weather is approaching as a low front nears. A low pressure area will bring with it cloudy and rainy weather. You can build your own barometer.

Do not build your barometer during a very high-pressure or low-pressure day. Prepare a straw as shown in Figure 28. Poke a pin through one end of a straw. Tape one end of a length of cotton thread to the same end of the straw. Tape another pin to the other end of the straw. This pin will serve as a pointer.

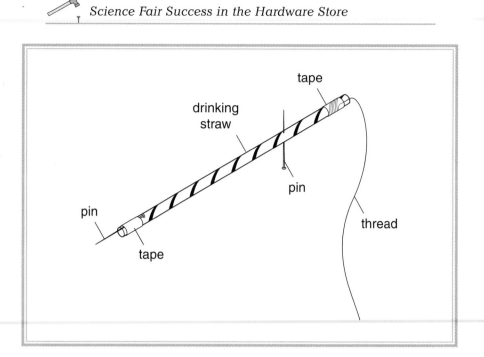

Figure 28. The straw will function as a gauge to indicate whether the atmospheric pressure is rising or falling. The needle taped to the end of the straw will serve as a pointer that indicates a rise or fall in atmospheric pressure.

Remove the lid from a large, empty container. A large cardboard box works well. Cover the top with plastic wrap and secure with an elastic band. Tape the free end of the cotton thread to the plastic wrap. Stand a piece of cardboard securely behind the container.

Push the pin that you pierced through the straw into the cardboard, as shown in Figure 29. Position the cardboard box so that the tension on the cotton string keeps the straw in a horizontal position, as shown in Figure 29.

Over the next several days, mark the cardboard to note the positions of the pin on the end of the straw. Your marks will form a dial. The top of the dial will indicate high pressure,

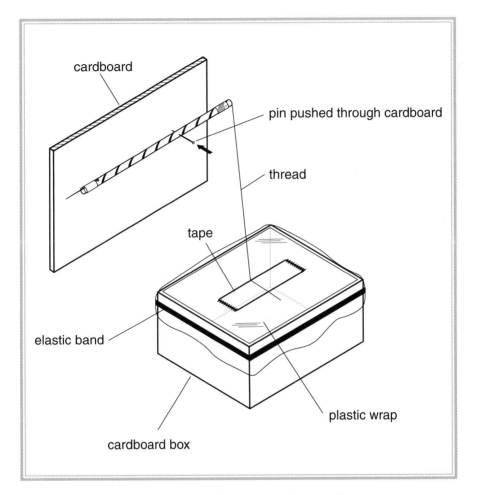

cardboard

pin pushed through cardboard

thread

tape

elastic band

cardboard box

plastic wrap

Figure 29. Once you have everything set up, make sure that no one moves the box or else your barometer will be inaccurate. Changes in barometric pressure will cause the plastic wrap covering the box to rise and fall. As it does, the string will cause the straw to move as it pivots on the pin. As the pointer (pin) on the end of the straw moves up and down, mark the corresponding points on the cardboard. You will then have a dial to note any change in barometric pressure.

and the bottom will indicate low pressure. You are now set to forecast the weather. As the atmospheric pressure rises, it pushes down on the plastic wrap. This increased pressure causes the straw to pivot upward. A decrease in atmospheric pressure causes the plastic wrap to move upward, allowing the straw to pivot downward. Compare your barometric changes with those of the weather forecaster on the radio or television. Did your barometer work?

Project Idea

Making a Different Kind of Weather Forecaster

An alternative to using a barometer is to use a chemical solution and filter paper to forecast the weather. Some chemicals change color, depending on whether or not they contain water. Such chemicals are known as hydrated salts. Use the library and the Internet to search for information on these salts. Choose one to prepare a solution that you can apply to filter paper. Apply several coats of solution, allowing the paper to dry between each application. Observe its color. Place the filter paper near an open window when it rains. Notice what happens to the color. Use what you learn to make a weather indicator to mount on the outside of your house. That way you will know what the weather should be like for your next family barbecue.

Experiment 5.2

How Can You Prove the Atmosphere Exerts Pressure?

Materials

* ✳ empty coffee can with plastic lid
* ✳ water
* ✳ hammer
* ✳ small nail
* ✳ masking tape

In the 1600s, people used a rather simple device that depended on atmospheric pressure to forecast the weather. The device was known as a "poor man's barometer" because it was inexpensive to make. This device, called a weather glass, became a standard ship's instrument for forecasting approaching storms. You can still find weather glasses in use today in a variety of places. No matter what instrument you use, you will find that the atmosphere is always exerting a pressure. This is a simple experiment to prove that the atmosphere continuously exerts a pressure.

With a hammer and a small nail, punch three small holes on the bottom of an empty coffee can and one small hole in the plastic lid. Cover the holes in the can with masking tape. Fill the coffee can halfway with water. Place the lid on the can. Hold the can over a sink. Remove the masking tape over the holes in the can. Place your finger over the hole in the lid and press down gently. Observe what happens.

Slowly stop applying pressure on the lid. Remove your finger from the hole in the lid. Observe what happens. When you filled the can halfway with water, the remaining space was filled with air. The water inside the can was under atmospheric pressure from two sources—one above the water, the

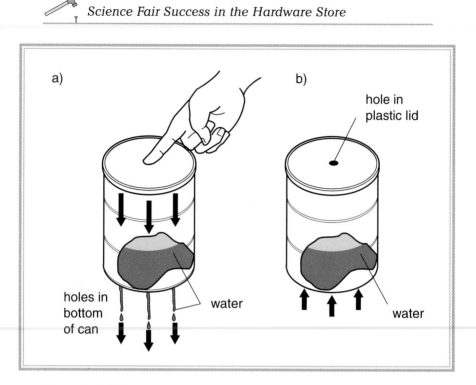

a)

b)

hole in
plastic lid

holes in
bottom
of can

water

water

Figure 30. a) Water pours out of the bottom of the can because of the higher pressure exerted on the water from above. b) Because the atmospheric pressure is the same both above and below the water, the water remains in the can.

other below the water. Pushing down on the lid increased the pressure on the air above the water. As shown in Figure 30a, this pressure above the water was high enough to overcome the pressure exerted by the atmosphere on the bottom of the water. Thus the water was forced out the bottom of the can.

When you removed your finger, you stopped putting pressure on the air that is above the water. But the atmospheric pressure outside continued to put pressure on the bottom of the water, keeping it inside the can, as shown in Figure 30b. How might these results be different if you performed the same experiment on top of Mount Everest, where the atmospheric pressure is much lower? Experiment to see if the number of holes affects how the water is forced out of the can when you apply pressure. You can also test whether placing holes in the side of the can produces the same result. For example, try punching holes vertically down one side of a coffee can. Be sure that all the holes you make will be below the level of the water that is placed in the can.

Experiment 5.3

Why Would Anyone Pour Baking Soda into a Swimming Pool?

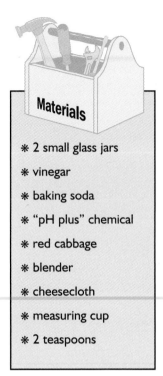

Materials

* 2 small glass jars
* vinegar
* baking soda
* "pH plus" chemical
* red cabbage
* blender
* cheesecloth
* measuring cup
* 2 teaspoons

In Chapter 1, you read about how acid precipitation can affect the pH of the soil and various bodies of water. Included among these bodies of water are pools. No matter whether the pool is a small, freestanding one or a large, inground one, the water can gradually become more acidic after each rainfall. Hardware stores sell chemicals to counteract this increased acidity of pool water. Why are these chemicals usually referred to as "pH plus" chemicals? In the following experiment, you can test the effectiveness of a "pH plus" chemical compared to that of a chemical you are likely to find in your kitchen cabinet—baking soda.

Prepare some red cabbage juice as described in Experiment 1.2. In each of two jars, mix one cup of vinegar with one ounce of red cabbage juice. Note the color of the solution.

Add one teaspoon of the "pH plus" chemical to one jar. Stir and observe the color. Add one teaspoon of baking soda to the other jar. Stir and observe the color. Continue adding known amounts of the "pH plus" chemical and baking soda to each jar until you notice an observable color change in each jar.

Recall from Chapter 1 that vinegar is an acidic solution. Both the "pH plus" chemical and baking soda will increase the pH of the vinegar solution, as evidenced by a color change. Thus both these chemicals counteract the effect of acid rain on pool water. The more effective chemical is the one that requires the smaller amount to raise the pH of the vinegar solution. Which one was that? Experiment with other household products to see which ones are as effective as the "pH plus" product.

Buffers

Like the water in a pool, your body contains both acids and bases. But unlike the water in a pool, your body will be seriously affected by even a slight change in the pH of your blood. The pH of human blood is slightly basic. If the blood pH were to change ever so slightly, serious problems would arise. For example, when the blood pH falls to less than 7.35, a person develops a condition called *acidosis*. A person with acidosis can faint and go into a coma if the condition persists. If the blood pH rises above 7.45, a condition called *alkalosis* develops. A person with alkalosis becomes overly excitable and nervous. If the condition persists, the person may also develop muscle spasms and convulsions.

Obviously, the body must have some mechanism to make sure that the blood pH does not change to any significant extent. Such a mechanism involves a buffer. A **buffer** is a chemical system that can withstand small additions of acid or base without a significant change in pH. You may have heard of buffered aspirin. Aspirin is an acid. Buffered aspirin contains chemicals that keep the stomach's pH from changing because of the acidity of the aspirin.

Experiment 5.4

How Can You Neutralize an Acid?

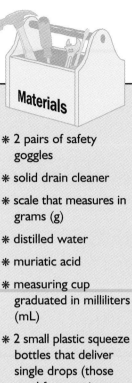

A strong acid can dissolve metals. A strong base can unclog a drain. But if you mix an acid and a base in just the right way, you get a salt solution that cannot melt metals or unclog drains. When this happens, the acid and base are said to have neutralized each other. A reaction in which an acid and a base are neutralized to produce a salt solution is called a **neutralization reaction**. You can carry out a neutralization reaction to determine the concentration of an acid or a base.

In this experiment, you can determine the concentration of an acid used to clean pools by neutralizing it with a base that is used to unclog drains. The procedure you will use is called a titration. A **titration** is a procedure in which a solution of known concentration is used to determine the concentration of a second, unknown solution. You will prepare a basic solution with a known concentration. You will then

Materials

* 2 pairs of safety goggles
* solid drain cleaner
* scale that measures in grams (g)
* distilled water
* muriatic acid
* measuring cup graduated in milliliters (mL)
* 2 small plastic squeeze bottles that deliver single drops (those used for carrying shampoo when traveling can be used)
* 2 laxative tablets that contain the ingredient phenolphthalein
* rubbing alcohol
* paper towel
* hammer
* wooden board
* small glass jar
* coffee filter
* tall drinking glass
* dropper
* an adult

use this solution to determine the concentration of an acid solution that is used to clean pools. This acid, called muriatic acid, is available from hardware stores. You will need **an adult** to prepare the muriatic acid solution that you will use in this experiment.

Put on a pair of safety goggles and ask an adult to do the same. Avoid direct contact with the base and acid solutions that you will use. If you do come in contact with any, immediately wash the area with running water.

Ask an adult to prepare a base solution of known concentration by adding 5 g of solid drain cleaner to a glass jar. Then add 95 mL of distilled water to the jar and stir the solution until all the drain cleaner has dissolved. You now have a 5 percent base solution that you will use to determine the concentration of the acid solution. Fill one of the plastic bottles with the 5 percent base solution and record its mass when filled. Use running water to rinse the glass jar used to make the base solution. Dry the jar for the next step.

Place two laxative tablets between the halves of a folded paper towel. Use a hammer to crush the tablets on a wooden board. Place the crushed tablets in the glass jar and add 25 mL of rubbing alcohol to dissolve the tablets. Fold a coffee filter as shown in Figure 31. Then place the folded filter in a tall drinking glass. Pour the alcohol solution through the filter. Clean the jar and save the filtrate that collects in the glass for the next step.

Ask an adult to mix 20 mL of muriatic acid with 100 mL of distilled water in a glass jar. Muriatic acid is available in hardware stores and is used to clean certain kinds of swimming pools. The diluted muriatic acid is the solution of unknown

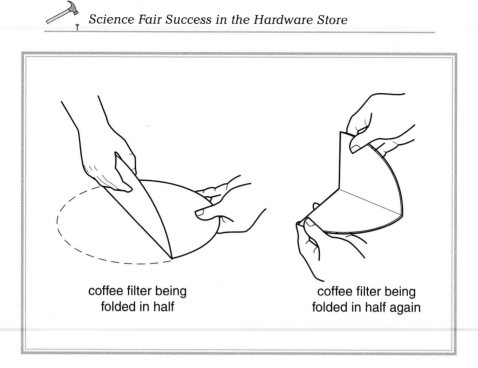

coffee filter being
folded in half

coffee filter being
folded in half again

Figure 31. Fold a coffee filter in half and then in half again. Then open the filter and insert it in a tall glass.

concentration. Fill a plastic bottle with the diluted muriatic acid solution and record its mass when filled. Clean and dry the glass jar. Pour about one third of the acid solution in the plastic bottle into the glass jar. Add 3 drops of the laxative/alcohol solution to the acid. The phenolphthalein in the laxative is an indicator. You read in Experiment 1.2 that an indicator changes color depending on whether the solution is an acid or a base. Phenolphthalein is colorless in an acidic solution. In a basic solution, phenolphthalein is pink.

Slowly add the base solution in the plastic bottle drop by drop to the acid in the jar. As you add each drop, continue to swirl the jar to mix the acid and base. Notice that a pink color appears when a drop of base is added but disappears upon swirling. Continue adding the base until one drop causes a pink color that persists for 30 seconds after swirling. At this point, you have reached the end of the titration.

Weigh both plastic bottles. Calculate the amount of acid you used by subtracting the mass of the bottle at the end of the titration from the mass of the bottle when it was full at the start of the experiment. Do the same to calculate the amount of base you added. The concentration of the acid solution is calculated by comparing the ratio of acid and base that were used. For example, if you used 25 g of acid and 25 g of base, their ratio is 1:1. Because the concentration of the base is 5 percent, then the concentration of the acid is also 5 percent. However, if you used twice as much base to neutralize the acid, then the ratio of base to acid is 2:1. Because you used twice as much base to neutralize the acid, the acid must be twice the concentration of the base. In this case, the acid concentration is 2 x 5 percent, or 10 percent. If you used half as much base to neutralize the acid, then the ratio of base to acid is 1:2. Because you use half as much base, the acid must be half the concentration of the base. In this case, the acid concentration is ½ x 5 percent, or 2.5 percent.

Under adult supervision, you can use this procedure to determine the concentration of the acid in various household solutions, including vinegar and club soda. Once you know the concentration of an acidic solution, you can use it to determine the concentration of a household solution that is basic, such as ammonia and toilet bowl cleaner. **Never mix ammonia and bleach.**

Experiment 5.5

Does Chlorine Really Clean?

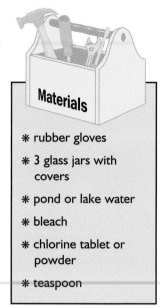

People with pools worry about not only the pH of the water but also its cleanliness. What they do not want to see is a green or brown scum that starts to form on the walls of the pool. This scum forms when algae or bacteria start to thrive and reproduce in the water. Algae are simple plantlike organisms that grow fast and carry out photosynthesis quite efficiently.

When conditions are just right, pool water offers algae and bacteria an excellent place to thrive. Chlorine is usually added to the water to prevent these organisms from forming and to kill any that have formed. Recall from Chapter 4 that chlorine is often added to drinking water to kill microorganisms that can cause disease. The chlorine added to pool water comes either in powder or tablet form, both of which are available at hardware stores.

Chlorine is also found in household bleach, usually in the form of sodium hypochlorite or calcium hypochlorite. In this case, the chlorine is used not only to kill disease-causing germs but also to remove stains from clothing. The chlorine reacts with the chemicals responsible for the stain. Once combined, the colored material is changed into a colorless compound. The chemicals that caused the stain are still in the clothing. They just cannot be seen because they have become colorless.

In this experiment, you will have the opportunity to test both household bleach and a chlorine product sold for pools for their ability to destroy disease-causing organisms. You may discover that ordinary bleach is just as effective and cheaper than a chlorine powder or tablet. Perhaps that is why many people pour some bleach into their pools when a serious algae problem develops.

Fill three glass jars with either pond or lake water. Make sure that the water is fairly clear. If not, pass it through a coffee filter. Cover your hands with a pair of rubber gloves. Add one teaspoon of bleach to one jar and stir. Take care not to spill any bleach on your hands or clothing. Place the cover on loosely and label the jar to show that bleach was added. Dissolve a quarter-teaspoon of chlorine powder in water. If you are using a chlorine tablet, first crush it to form a powder. Do not touch the powdered chlorine. Add one teaspoon of chlorinated water to the other jar, stir, and cover loosely. Label the jar to show that chlorine was added. To a third jar, add nothing to the water. Set the jars in sunlight and observe them over the next two weeks.

At the end of the first week, add another teaspoon of bleach to the first jar and another teaspoon of powdered chlorine to the second jar. If the bleach or powdered chlorine was effective, then the water should remain clear. But if the water turns cloudy, or if a green, brown, or red scum forms inside the jar, then algae and other tiny organisms survived and reproduced. If this happens, you may want to repeat the experiment using more bleach and chlorine powder. On the other hand, if nothing grew in either jar, then you may want to decrease the quantity of bleach and chlorine powder you used.

Keep in mind that chlorine eventually breaks down in water. That is why it must be added to pools on a weekly basis and why you added more bleach and chlorine to the jars after the first week.

Project Idea

Using Chlorine to Kill Bacteria

You can expand upon the experiment with bleach and turn it into a project. Check the effectiveness of bleach and a chlorine pool product in killing bacteria. In Chapter 4, you may have carried out the project on bacteria in water supplies. If you did, then you know how to culture bacteria in petri dishes. If not, you will need to learn certain techniques that are used in microbiology. As part of this project, you can also investigate the chemistry of bleaches. Bleaches can function in both oxidation and reduction reactions. You can compare the chemistry of these two processes, showing how both oxidizing and reducing bleaches work.

Experiment 5.6

How Can You Make a Reaction Happen Faster?

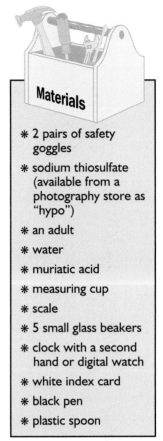

Materials

* 2 pairs of safety goggles
* sodium thiosulfate (available from a photography store as "hypo")
* an adult
* water
* muriatic acid
* measuring cup
* scale
* 5 small glass beakers
* clock with a second hand or digital watch
* white index card
* black pen
* plastic spoon

The first time an inground pool is opened for the season, the water may actually be green. This happens because the algae were able to reproduce so much that they caused the water to turn green. Adding chlorine at this point might not solve the problem. In that case, a chemical must be added that will kill the algae by starving them of the minerals they need. The chemical that is added is called aluminum sulfate. Commonly known as alum, this chemical can be found in hardware stores that sell pool supplies.

Gunite pools are inground pools whose walls are made of concrete. Obviously, one advantage they offer is a longer life expectancy. One disadvantage is a tendency to become encrusted with dirt and grime even after only one season of use. When this happens, the water must be drained from the pool and the walls cleaned with a muriatic acid solution. You can also use muriatic acid to see how you can make a chemical reaction happen faster.

Throughout this book, you have had the chance to examine a number of chemical reactions. You may have placed galvanized nails in vinegar and watched them react to produce gas bubbles. Or you may have used two metals and observed them react to generate electricity. No matter what the reaction is, in most cases, you can make it happen faster. One way is to vary the quantities of the materials you mix to react.

Put on a pair of safety goggles and ask an adult to do the same. **Have the adult** dilute the muriatic acid with an equal volume of water. Be sure to add the acid to the water. Further dilute the acid by dissolving 1 ounce of the diluted muriatic acid in 1 quart of distilled water.

Label the glass beakers from *1* to *5*. Fill each beaker as shown in Table 3. Note that the total volume in each beaker is 5 fluid ounces.

Print your name in black ink on a white index card. Place beaker 1 over your name. Add 1 ounce of the diluted muriatic acid to beaker 1. Begin timing as soon as you add the muriatic acid. Stir the solution at a steady rate with a plastic spoon until you can no longer see your name through the

Table 3. Contents of experimental beakers *1–5*

Beaker number	Volume of sodium thiosulfate (fluid ounces)	Volume of distilled water (fluid ounces)
1	5	0
2	4	1
3	3	2
4	2	3
5	1	4

solution in the beaker. Record how long it takes until you can no longer see your name through the solution. Place the index card under beaker 2, add 1 ounce of muriatic acid, stir, and start timing. Do the same with beakers 3–5.

As the reaction between the sodium thiosulfate and muriatic acid proceeds, the solution becomes cloudy. This happens because the reaction produces a solid material known as a *precipitate*. Make a graph of your data by plotting the time in seconds for each reaction on the y-axis and volume of sodium thiosulfate in fluid ounces on the x-axis. What is the relationship between the volume of sodium thiosulfate used in this experiment and the time it takes for the reaction? Do your results support the fact that concentration affects the rate of a reaction? How would you modify this experiment so that you investigate the effect of changing the concentration of muriatic acid?

Glossary

acid—Chemical that produces a solution with a pH value less than 7.

adsorb—To take up and hold, as soil does with water.

alloy—Mixture of two or more metals that can exist either as a solid or a liquid.

atom—Building block of all matter.

barometric pressure—Pressure exerted by the atmosphere that supports a column of mercury.

base—Chemical that produces a solution with a pH value larger than 7.

buffer—Chemical system that can withstand a small addition of an acid or base without undergoing a significant change in pH.

capacitor—Device that can store electrical energy.

chemical bond—Force of attraction between two atoms.

colloid—Particle that is too large to dissolve in a solution but too small to settle to the bottom.

conductor—Object or chemical that conducts electricity.

control—Experimental design that allows only one factor to determine the results.

deionized water—Water that is free, or relatively free, of dissolved salts.

density—Ratio of mass to volume.

dependent variable—Factor in an experiment that changes as a result of what is done.

distillation—Process used to isolate a pure liquid.

distilled water—100 percent pure water.

electricity—Form of energy generated by the flow of electrons.

electrolysis—Use of electrical energy to produce a chemical change.

electrolyte—Anything in solution that conducts an electric current.

electrolytic cell—Device that converts electrical energy into chemical energy.

electron—Negatively charged particle that orbits the nucleus of an atom.

electroplating—Use of electrical energy to coat an object with a pure metal.

ferromagnetic—Term characterizing an object or chemical that retains its magnetic properties.

filtrate—Liquid that passes through a filter.

fractional distillation—Process used to separate the various liquids in a mixture based on their different boiling points.

galvanic cell—Device that converts chemical energy into electrical energy.

galvanization—Process of using a metal to coat another metal.

hydrocarbon—Organic compound made of carbon and hydrogen atoms.

independent variable—Factor that the experimenter is free to add or change as part of the procedure.

indicator—Chemical whose color depends on the pH of the solution.

inorganic compound—With few exceptions, a chemical compound that lacks the element carbon.

insulator—Object or chemical that does not conduct electricity.

ion—Charged particle that forms when an atom either loses or gains an electron.

leaching—The process of dissolving and washing out nutrients.

loam—Soil that contains the ideal mixture of substances for growing plants.

microbiology—Study of tiny organisms such as bacteria and viruses.

neutralization reaction—Reaction between an acid and a base that produces a salt and water.

neutron—Neutral particle in the nucleus of an atom.

organic compound—With few exceptions, a chemical compound that contains the element carbon.

oxidation—Loss of electrons by a chemical substance.

paramagnetic—Term characterizing an object or chemical that can lose its magnetic properties.

pH—Measurement of the relative concentration of an acid or base.

pheromone—Chemical that is released by an animal to communicate with others through scent or taste.

proton—Positively charged particle in the nucleus of an atom.

redox reaction—Reaction that involves both oxidation and reduction.

reduction—Gain of electrons by a substance.

static electricity—Spontaneous jumping of electrons from one object to another.

titration—Procedure in which a solution of known concentration is used to determine the concentration of a second unknown solution.

Tyndall effect—Scattering of light by colloids in a liquid. A light beam is visible as it passes through the liquid.

variable—Factor that can change during an experiment.

voltage—"Electrical pressure" created by a flow of electrons.

Further Reading

Books

Bochinski, Julianne Blair. *The Complete Handbook of Science Fair Projects.* New York: John Wiley and Sons, 1996.

Bonnet, Bob, and Dan Keen. *Science Fair Projects with Electricity and Electronics.* New York: Sterling Publications, 1996.

Brisk, Marion A. *1,001 Ideas for Science Projects.* Paramus, N.J.: Prentice Hall, 1994.

Friedhoffer, Robert. *Physics Lab in a Hardware Store.* Danbury, Conn.: Franklin Watts, 1996.

Gardner, Robert. *Science Projects About Kitchen Chemistry.* Springfield, N.J.: Enslow Publishers, Inc., 1999.

———. *Science Projects About Electricity and Magnets.* Springfield, N.J.: Enslow Publishers, Inc., 1994.

Newton, David. *Making and Using Scientific Equipment.* Danbury, Conn.: Franklin Watts, 1993.

Ronan, Colin A., ed. *Science Explained: The World of Science in Everyday Life.* Las Vegas, Nev.: Henry Holt & Company, 1995.

Tocci, Salvatore. *How to Do a Science Fair Project.* Danbury, Conn.: Franklin Watts, 1997.

———. *Science Fair Success Using Supermarket Products.* Berkeley Heights, N.J.: Enslow Publishers, Inc., 2000.

Vecchione, Glen. *100 Amazing Make-It-Yourself Science Fair Projects.* New York: Sterling Publications, 1997.

Wong, Ovid. *Experimenting With Electricity and Magnetism.* Danbury, Conn.: Franklin Watts, 1993.

Internet Addresses

American Chemical Society

http://www.acs.org/

> *The society publishes a magazine called* ChemMatters *that focuses on the fun and practical applications of chemistry.*

California Energy Commission

http://www.energy.ca.gov/education

> *This site has a link to science projects. Each project has a short description with a link to the actual activity. Some activities have to be downloaded or printed with your Web browser software.*

Hands-On-Science Organization

http://www.hands-on-science.org/

> *One section is devoted to "Kids" with information on things to do at home and an opportunity to provide feedback.*

Information Unlimited

http://www.amazing1.com/

> *This company sells plans for constructing a variety of items, including how to make a scrap-metal battery, grow bacteria and fungi at home, and construct an electronic air purifier.*

SciCentral

http://scicentral.com

> *This site is a science and engineering metadirectory that is maintained by professional scientists. One link leads to a K–12 science page with a science fair project resource guide.*

List of Suppliers

Scientific supply companies usually sell their merchandise only to schools and not to individuals. Thus, you may need to check with your science teacher if you need a chemical or special piece of glassware that is not available at home. Your school may have the item that you need. If not, ask your teacher for a catalog from one of these companies. By looking through the catalog, you may get ideas on how to come up with your own substitute for a piece of equipment or glassware that is not only cheaper but also reflects your creativity. This will not only help you to carry out your project, but will also serve to impress anyone who takes the time to look at it. Two companies where you can order supplies directly and have them mailed to your home are:

Edmund Scientific
101 E. Gloucester Pike
Barrington, NJ 08007
1-609-573-6250
1-609-547-3488

Educational Innovations, Inc.
151 River Road
Cos Cob, CT 06807-2514
http://www.teachersource.com

Index